Edmond About

The King of the Mountains

Edmond About

The King of the Mountains

ISBN/EAN: 9783743341067

Manufactured in Europe, USA, Canada, Australia, Japa

Cover: Foto ©ninafisch / pixelio.de

Manufactured and distributed by brebook publishing software (www.brebook.com)

Edmond About

The King of the Mountains

THE
KING OF THE MOUNTAINS

BY EDMUND ABOUT.

TRANSLATED FROM THE FRENCH BY
MRS. C. A. KINGSBURY.

CHICAGO AND NEW YORK:
RAND, McNALLY & COMPANY.
MDCCCXCVII.

THE KING OF THE MOUNTAINS.

I.

HERMANN SCHULTZ.

On the 3d of July, about six o'clock in the morning, I was watering my flowers. A young man entered the garden. He was blonde, beardless; he wore a German cap and sported gold spectacles. A long, loose woolen coat, or paletot, drooped in a melancholy way around his form, like a sail around a mast in a calm. He wore no gloves; his tan leather shoes had such large soles, that the foot was surrounded by a narrow flange. In the breast-pocket of his paletot, a huge porcelain pipe bulged half-way out. I did not stop to ask myself whether this young man was a student in the German Universities; I put down my watering-pot, and saluted him with: "Guten Morgen!"

"Monsieur," he said to me in French, but with a deplorable accent, "my name is Hermann Schultz; I have come to pass some months in Greece, and I have carried your book with me everywhere."

This praise penetrated my heart with sweet joy; the stranger's voice seemed more melodious than Mozart's music, and I directed toward his gold glasses a swift look of gratitude. You would scarcely believe, dear reader, how much we love those who have taken the trouble to decipher our jargon. As for me, if I have ever sighed to be rich, it is in order to assure an income to all those who have read my works.

I took him by the hand, this excellent young man. I seated him beside me on the garden-bench. He told me that he was a botanist, that he had a commission from the "Jardin des Plantes" in Hamburg. In order to complete his herbarium he was studying the country, the animals, and the people. His naive descriptions, his terse but just decisions, recalled to me, a little, the simple old Herodotus. He expressed himself awkwardly, but with a candor which inspired confidence; he emphasized his words with the tone of a man entirely convinced. He questioned me, if not of every one in Athens, at least of all the principal personages in my book. In the course of the conversation, he made some statements on general subjects, which seemed to me far more reasonable than any which I had advanced. At the end of an hour we had become good friends.

I do not know which of us first spoke of brigandage. People who travel in Italy talk of paintings; those who visit England talk of manufactures; each country has its specialty.

"My dear sir," I asked of my guest, "have you met any brigands? Is it true, as is reported, that there are still bandits in Greece?"

"It is only too true," he gravely replied. "I was for fifteen days in the hands of the terrible Hadgi-Stavros, nicknamed The King of the Mountains. I speak then from experience. If you have leisure, and a long story will not weary you, I am ready to give you the details of my adventure. You may make of it what you please; a romance, a novel, or perhaps an additional chapter in the little book in which you have written so many curious facts."

"You are very good," I replied, "and I am at your disposal. Let us go to my study. It is cooler there than in the garden and yet we can enjoy the odor of the sweet-peas and mignonette."

He followed me, humming to himself in Greek, a popular song:

> "A robber with black eyes descends to the plains;
> His gun is heard at each step;
> He says to the vultures: 'Do not leave me,
> I will serve to you the Pasha of Athens.'"

He seated himself on a divan, with his legs crossed under him like the Arabian story-tellers, took off his loose paletot, lighted his pipe and began his tale. I seated myself at my desk and took stenographic notes as he dictated.

I have always been without much distrust, especially with those who have complimented me. Sometimes the amiable stranger told me such surprising things that I asked myself many times if he was not mocking me. But his manner was so simple, his blue eyes so limpid, that my suspicions faded away on the instant.

He talked steadily, until half after noon. He stopped two or three times only long enough to re-light his pipe.

He smoked with regular puffs like the smoke stack of a steam-engine. Each time I raised my eyes, I beheld him, calm, smiling, in the midst of a thick cloud of smoke, like Jupiter in the 5th act of Amphitryon.

We were interrupted by a servant with the announcement that breakfast was served. Hermann seated himself opposite me, and my trifling suspicions vanished before his appetite. I said to myself that a good digestion rarely accompanies a bad conscience. The young German was too good an eater to be an untruthful narrator, and his veracity restored my faith in his veracity. Struck with this idea, I confessed, while offering him some strawberries, that I had, for an instant, doubted him. He replied with an angelic smile.

I passed the entire day with my new friend, and I found that the time did not drag. At five o'clock, he knocked the ashes from his pipe, put on his outer coat, and shaking my hand, said: "Adieu." I replied: "Au revoir."

"No," he said, shaking his head; "I leave to-night at seven o'clock, and I dare not hope ever to see you again."

"Leave your address. I have not yet renounced the pleasure of traveling, and I may, sometime, pass through Hamburg."

"Unfortunately, I do not know where I shall pitch my tent. Germany is large; I may not remain a citizen of Hamburg."

"But if I publish your story, at least I ought to send you a copy."

"Do not take that trouble. As soon as the book is published, it will appear in Leipzig and I will read it. Adieu!"

After his departure, I re-read attentively what I had written. I found some remarkable details, but nothing which contradicts what I had seen and heard during my stay in Greece.

At the moment of finishing the manuscript, a scruple restrained me: What if some errors had crept into Hermann's statements? In my quality of editor was I not responsible? To publish the story of "The King of the Mountains," was it not to expose myself to editorial comments and criticisms?

In my perplexity, I thought of making a copy of the original. I sent the first to M. Pseftis. I begged him to point out, candidly, all the errors, and I promised to print his reply at the end of the volume.

I re-read the copy which I had retained. I changed no word in it. If I made myself the corrector of the young German's statements, I would become his collaborator. So I discreetly withdrew. It is Hermann who speaks to you.

II.

PHOTINI.

You divine, from the appearance of my clothes, that I have not ten thousand francs with me. My father is an inn-keeper whom the railroads have ruined. In prosperous times he eats bread, in bad years potatoes. Add to this, that there are six children, all with good appetites. The day on which I received my commission from the Jardin des Plantes, there was a festival given in the family. My departure would not only increase the portion of each of my brothers, but I was to have two hundred and fifty francs per month and the expenses for my journey. It was a fortune. From that moment they ceased to call me Doctor. They dubbed me beef-merchant, so that I should appear rich! My brothers prophesied that I would be elected Professor by the University, on my return from Athens. My father hoped that I would return married. In his position of inn-keeper, he had assisted in some very romantic adventures. He cited, at least three times a week, the marriage of the Princess Ypsoff and Lieutenant Reynauld. The Princess occupied the finest apartments, with her two maids and her Courier, and she gave twenty florins a day. The French Lieutenant was in No. 17, way up under the eaves, and he paid a florin and a half, food included; however, after a month's sojourn at the hotel, he departed in a carriage with the Russian lady.

My poor father, with the partiality of a father, thought that I was handsomer and more elegant than Lieutenant Reynauld; he did not doubt but that, sooner or later, I would meet a princess who would enrich us all. If I did not find her at a table d'hote, I would see her in a railway carriage. If the powers which control the railroads were not propitious, there was still left the steamships. The evening of my departure, we drank a bottle of old Rhine wine, and by chance the last was poured into my glass. The good man wept with joy: it was a sure sign, and nothing could prevent me from marrying within a year. I respected his superstitions, and I refrained from saying that princesses rarely travel third class. As for lodgings, my humble luggage would not permit me to choose any but modest inns, and royal families do not, usually, lodge in them. The fact is, that I landed in Greece without an adventure of any kind.

The army occupying the city made everything very dear in Athens. The Hotel d'Angleterre, the Hotel Orient, the Hotel des Etrangers were inaccessible. The Chancellor of the Prussian Legation, to whom I had brought a letter of introduction, was kind enough to assist me in finding a lodging. He took me to a pastry-cook's, at the corner of the Rue d'Hermes and the Place du Palais. I found there, board and lodging for a hundred francs a month. Christodule was an old Palikar, decorated with the Iron Cross, in memory of the War of Independence. He was a Lieutenant in the Phalanx, he wore the National costume, the red bonnet with blue tassel, the silver-colored vest, the white skirt, and the fancy leggins, when he sold ices and cakes. His wife, Maroula, was enormous, like all Greek women who have passed fifty. Her husband had purchased her during the war, when women sold for high prices. She was born in the Isle of Hydra, but she dressed in the Athenian fashion: upper garment or jacket of black velvet, skirt of a bright color, a silk handkerchief tied over her head. Neither Christodule nor his wife knew a word of German; but their son Dimitri, who was a servant hired by the day, and who dressed like a Frenchman, understood and spoke a little of each patois of Europe. Upon the whole, I had really no need of an interpreter. Without having received the gift of tongues, I am a fairly good linguist, and I murder Greek as readily as English, Italian or French.

My hosts were worthy people; they gave me a little white-washed room, with a table of white wood, two straw-bottomed chairs, a good but thin mattress, and some cotton quilts. A wooden bed is a superfluity which the Greeks easily deny themselves, and we lived a la Grecque. I breakfasted on a cup of arrow-root; I dined on a plate of meat with many olives, and dry fish; I supped on vegetables, honey and cakes. Preserves were not rare in the house, and occasionally I evoked memories of home by dining on a leg of lamb and preserves. It is useless to tell you that I had my pipe, and that the tobacco in Athens is better than yours. That which contributed to my feeling perfectly at home in Christodule's house, was a light wine of Santorin, which he bought, I know not where. I am not a judge of wines, and the education of my palate has, unfortunately, been neglected, but I believe, however, that this wine is worthy of a place on a king's table: it is of a fine topaz color, sparkling as the smile of a child. I see it now, in its large bulging carafe, on the shining linen cloth. It lighted the table and we were able to sup without any other illumination. I never drank much of it, because it was heady; and yet, at the end of a meal, I have recited some of Anacreon's verses and I have discovered remains of beauty in the moon-shaped face of the gross Maroula.

I ate with Christodule and his family. There were four regular boarders and one table boarder. The first floor was divided into four rooms, the best of which was occupied by a French Archaeologist, M. Hippolyte Mérinay. If all Frenchmen resemble this one, you would be a sorry lot. He was very small; his age, as far as one could tell, anywhere between eighteen and forty-five, very red-haired, very mild, very loquacious, and never loosening his moist and warm hands, when he had once fastened them on a person, until he had exhausted himself talking. His two dominant passions were archaeology and philanthropy: he was a member of many literary societies and of many benevolent associations. Although he was an advocate of charity, and his parents had left him a fine income, I do not remember ever to have seen him give a sou to a beggar. As for his knowledge of archaeology, I believe that it was of more account than his love for humanity. He had received a prize from some provincial College, for a treatise on the value of paper in the time of Orpheus. Encouraged by these first successes, he had come to Greece to gather material for a more important work: it was nothing less than to determine the quantity of oil consumed in Demosthenes' lamp while he wrote the second Philippic.

My two other neighbors were not so wise, and ancient things disturbed them not at all. Giacomo Fondi was a poor Maltese employed at, I know not what consulate; he earned a hundred and fifty francs a month sealing letters. I imagine that any other employment would have pleased him better. Nature, who has peopled the Island of Malta in order that the Orient should never lack porters, had given to poor Fondi the shoulders, arms and hands of a Milo of Crotona: he was born to handle a club, and not to melt sealing-wax with which to seal letters. He used, however, two or three sticks every day: man is not the master of his destiny! The islander out of his sphere, was in his element only at meal-time; he helped Maroula to place the table, and you will understand, without being told, that he always carried it at arms-length. He ate like the hero of the Iliad, and I shall never forget the cracking of his huge jaws, the dilation of his nostrils, the flash of his eyes, the whiteness of his thirty-two teeth, formidable mill-stones of which he was the mill. I ought to confess that I remember little of his conversation; one easily found the limit of his intelligence, but one never found the bounds of his appetite. Christodule had never made anything during the four years he had boarded him, although the Maltese had paid ten francs a month extra. The insatiable islander ate every day, after dinner, an enormous plateful of nuts, which he cracked between his first finger and thumb. Christodule, old soldier, but practical man, followed this exercise with a mixture of admiration and fear; he trembled for his dessert, yet he was proud to see, at his table, so huge a nut-cracker. The face of Giacomo Fondi would not have been out of place in one of the jumping-jack boxes, which so amuse children. It was whiter than a negro's; but it was a question of shade only. His thick locks descended to his eye-brows like a cap. In strange contrast, this Caliban had a very small foot, a slender ankle, a fine-shaped leg and as perfect as one finds in a statue; but these were details which one scarcely noticed. For whoever had seen him eat, his person began at the edge of the table; the rest of the body counted for nothing.

I can speak only from memory of William Lobster. He was a cherub of twenty years, blonde, rosy and chubby, but a cherub of the United States of America. The firm of Lobster and Sons, New York, had sent him to the Orient to study the subject of exportation. He worked during the day in the house of Philips Brothers; in the evening, he read Emerson; in the early morning or at sunrise he went to Socrates' school to practice pistol-shooting.

The most interesting person in our little colony was without doubt, John Harris, the maternal uncle of the little Lobster. The first time that I dined with this strange man, I was greatly taken with the American.

He was born at Vandalia, Illinois. Breathing the invigorating air of the new world from his birth, his every movement was joyous. I do not know whether the Harris family was rich or poor; whether the son went to College, or whether he educated himself. What was certain was, that at twenty-eight he relied on himself alone; was astonished at nothing; believed nothing impossible; never flinched; was amenable to reason; hoped for the best; attempted everything; triumphed in everything! If he fell, he immediately jumped up; if he stammered, he began all over again; he gave himself no rest; never lost courage, and went right ahead. He was well-educated, had been teacher, lawyer, journalist, miner, farmer, clerk. He had read everything, seen everything, tried everything, and had traveled over more than half of the globe. When I made his acquaintance he was commanding a Dispatch-boat, carrying sixty men and four cannons. He wrote of the Orient in the Boston Review; he transacted business with an indigo house in Calcutta, and yet he found time to come, four or five times a week, to dine with his nephew, Lobster, and with us.

A single instance, of a thousand, will serve to show his character. Early in the fifties he was in business in Philadelphia. His nephew, who was then seventeen, made him a visit. He found him near Washington Square, standing with his hands in his pockets, before a burning building. William touched him on the shoulder; he turned.

"Ah: Good-morning, Bill, thou hast arrived inopportunely, my boy. There is a fire which ruins me; I have forty thousand dollars in that house; we will not save a match."

"What will you do?" asked the astonished boy.

"What will I do? It is eleven o'clock, I am hungry, I have a little money in my pocket; I am going to take you to breakfast."

Harris was one of the most slender and most elegant men I have ever seen. He had a manly air, a fine forehead, a clear and proud eye.

Americans are never deformed nor mean-looking, and do you know why? Because they are not bound in the swaddling-clothes of a narrow civilization. Their minds and their bodies develop at will; their schoolroom is the open air; their master, exercise; their nurse, liberty.

I never cared especially for M. Mérinay; I looked at Giacomo Fondi with the indifferent curiosity with which one gazes at foreign animals; the little Lobster inspired me with luke-warm interest; but I conceived a warm affection for Harris. His frank face, his simple manners, his sternness which was not without sweetness, his hasty yet chivalrous temper, the oddities of his humor, the enthusiasm of his sentiments, appealed to me more strongly as I was neither enthusiastic nor hasty. We admire in others what we lack ourselves. Giacomo wore white clothes because he was black; I adore Americans because I am a German. As for the Greeks, I knew little of them even after four months' sojourn in their country. Nothing is easier than living in Athens without coming in contact with the natives. I did not go to a café; I did not read the

Pandore, nor the Minerve; nor any other paper of the country; I did not go to the theater, because I have a sensitive ear and a false note hurts me more cruelly than a blow; I lived with my hosts, my herbarium, and with John Harris. I could have presented myself at the Palace, thanks to my diplomatic pass-port and my official title. I had sent my card to the Master and Mistress of Ceremonies, and I could count upon an invitation to the first Court Ball. I kept in reserve for this occasion, a beautiful red coat, embroidered with silver, which my Aunt Rosenthaler had given to me the night before my departure. It was her husband's uniform; he was an assistant in a Scientific Institute, and prepared the specimens. My good aunt, a woman of great sense, knew that a uniform was well received in all countries, above all if it was red. My elder brother had remarked that I was larger than my uncle, as the sleeves were too short; but Papa quickly replied, that only the silver embroidery would catch the eye, and that princesses would not examine the uniform closely.

Unfortunately, the Court was not dancing that season. The winter pleasures were the flowering of almond, peach, and lemon trees. There was a vague report of a ball to be given the 15th of May; it made a stir in the city, as a few semi-official journals took it up; but there was nothing positively known about it.

My studies kept pace with my pleasures, slowly. I knew, by heart, the Botanical Gardens of Athens; they were neither very beautiful nor very full; it was a subject soon mastered. The Royal Gardens offered far more to study: an intelligent Frenchman had collected for it all the riches of the vegetable kingdom, from the palms of the West Indies to the saxifrage of the North. I passed whole days there studying M. Barraud's collections. The garden is public only at certain hours; but I spoke Greek to the guards, and for love of the Greek, they permitted me to enter. M. Barraud did not seem to weary of my company; he took me everywhere for the pleasure of discussing Botany and speaking French. In his absence, I hunted up the head gardener and questioned him in German: it is well to be polyglot.

I searched for plants every day in the surrounding country, but never as far from the city as I should like to have gone; there were many brigands around Athens. I am not a coward, the following story will prove it to you, but I love my life. It is a present which I received from my parents; I wish to preserve it as long as possible, in remembrance of my father and mother. In the month of April, 1856, it was dangerous to go far from the city: it was even imprudent to live outside. I did not venture upon the slopes of Lycabettus without thinking of poor Mme. Daraud who was robbed in broad day-light. The hills of Daphne recalled to me the capture of two French officers. Upon the road to Piraeus, I thought, involuntarily, of the band of brigands who traveled in six carriages as if on a pleasure tour, and who shot at passers by from the coach doors. The road to Pentelicus recalled the stopping of the Duchess de Plaisance, or the recent story of Harris and Lobster's adventure. They were returning from an excursion, on two Persian horses belonging to Harris, when they fell into an ambuscade. Two brigands, weapons in hand, stopped them in the middle of a bridge. They glanced all around and saw at their feet, in a ravine, a dozen rascals, armed to the teeth, who were guarding fifty or sixty prisoners. All who had passed that way since sunrise had been despoiled, then bound, so that no one could escape to give the alarm. Harris and his nephew were unarmed. Harris said to the young man in English: "Give up your money; it will not pay to be killed for twenty dollars." The brigands took the money, without letting go the bridles; they then showed the Americans the ravine and signed to them to descend. Harris now lost patience; it was repugnant to him to be bound; he was not the kind of wood of which one makes fagots. He looked at the little Lobster, and at the same instant, two fist blows like two chain-shots, struck the heads of the two brigands. William's adversary fell over on his back, at the same time, discharging his pistol; Harris' brigand, struck more forcibly, toppled over the cliff and fell among his comrades. Harris and Lobster were by this time quite a distance away, jamming the spurs into their horses. The band rose as one man and discharged their weapons. The horses were killed, the young men disengaged themselves, took to their heels, and when they reached the city, warned the police, who started in pursuit of the brigands the second morning after.

Our excellent Christodule learned with grief of the

death of the two horses; but he found not a word of blame for the killers. "What would you have?" he asked with charming simplicity, "it is their business." All Greeks are, more or less, of our host's opinion. It is not that the brigands spare their countrymen and reserve their harshness for strangers, but a Greek, robbed by his brother, says to himself with a certain resignation, that the money is all in the family. The populace sees itself plundered by the brigands, as a woman of the people who is beaten by her husband, admires him because he strikes hard. Native moralists complained of the excesses committed in the country, as a father deplores his son's pranks. He groans loudly, but secretly admires him; he would be ashamed if he was like his neighbor's son who never had to be spoken to.

It was a fact, that at the time of my arrival, the hero of Athens was the scourge of Attica. In the salons and in the cafés, in the barber-shops where the common people congregated, at the pharmacies where the bourgeoise were to be found, in the muddy streets of the bazars, in the dusty square of Belle-Gréce, at the theater, at the Sunday concerts, and upon the road to Patissia, one heard only of the great Hadgi-Stavros; one swore only by Hadgi-Stavros; Hadgi-Stavros the invincible, Hadgi-Stavros the terror of the police, Hadgi-Stavros, "The King of the Mountains!" They almost composed (God pardon me) a litany on Hadgi-Stavros.

One Sunday, a little while after his adventure, John Harris dined with us; I started Christodule upon the subject of Hadgi-Stavros. Our host had often visited him, years before, during the War of Independence, when brigandage was less discussed than now.

He emptied his glass of Sautorin, stroked his gray mustache, and began a long recital, interspersed with many sighs. He informed us that Stavros was the son of a bishop or priest of the Greek Church, in the island of Tino. He was born God knew in what year; Greeks of early times knew not their ages, because registries of the civil state are an invention of the decadence. His father, who destined him for the Church, taught him to read. When about twenty years of age, he made a pilgrimage to Jerusalem, and added to his name the title, Hadgi; which means, pilgrim. Hadgi-Stavros, returning to his own country, was taken prisoner by a pirate. The conqueror found him amenable to reason and make a sailor of him. Thus he began to make war on Turkish ships, and, generally, on those which had not mounted guns. At the end of several years, he tired of working for others, and determined to push out for himself. He possessed neither boat, nor money to buy one; necessity compelled him to practice piracy on land. The rising of the Greeks against Turkey permitted him to fish in troubled waters. He never could tell exactly whether he was a brigand or an insurgent; whether he commanded a band of thieves or insurrectionists. His hatred of the Turks did not blind him to the degree that he could pass a Greek village without seeing it and sacking it. All money was good to him, whether it came from friend or foe, from a simple theft or a glorious pillage.

Such wise impartiality rapidly increased his fortune. The shepherds hastened to place themselves under his banner, when they learned that good pay might be expected; his reputation brought him an army. The leaders of the insurrection knew of his exploits, but not of his thrift: in those times, one saw only the bright side of everything. Lord Byron dedicated an ode to him; poets and orators in Paris compared him to Epaminondas, and even to poor Aristides. Some sent him embroidered clothes from the Faubourg Saint-Germain; others sent subsidies. He received money from France, from England and from Russia; I will not swear that he never received any from Turkey: he was a true Palikar! At the end of the war, he was besieged, with other chiefs, in the Acropolis at Athens. He slept in the propyleum, between Margaritis and Lygandas, and each had his treasure hid in the blanket which covered him. One summer night, the roof fell so cleverly that it killed every one but Hadgi-Stavros, who was smoking his pipe in the open air. He secured his companions' money and every one thought that he well deserved it. But a misfortune which he had not foreseen checked his successful career: peace was declared. Hadgi-Stavros retired to the country with his spoils, and became a spectator of strange occurrences. The powers which had freed Greece attempted to found a kingdom. Some offensive words came buzzing around the hairy ears of the old robber; he heard rumors of government—of armies—of public order. He laughed when told that his possessions were included in one sub-prefecture. But when an employée from the

Treasury presented himself to collect the yearly taxes, he became serious. He threw the man out of the door, not without having relieved him of all he had brought with him. Justice sought to punish him; he took to the mountains. It was as well, for he was tired of his house. He felt, to a certain extent, that he owned a roof, but on condition that he slept above it.

His former companions-in-arms had scattered all over the kingdom. The State had given them lands; they cultivated them reluctantly and ate sparingly of the bitter bread of labor. When they learned that their chief was at variance with the law, they sold their farms and hastened to join him. As for the brigand, he rented his lands: he had the qualifications of an administrator.

Peace and idleness had made him ill and unhappy. The mountain air restored his cheerfulness and health, so that in 1840 he thought of marriage. He was, assuredly, past fifty, but men of his temper have nothing to do with old age; death, even, looks at them twice before it attacks them. He married an heiress with a magnificent dowry, from one of the best families in Laconia, and thus became allied to the highest personages of the kingdom. His wife followed him everywhere. After giving birth to a daughter, she took a fever and died. He brought up the child himself, with all the care and tenderness of a mother. When the brigands saw him dancing the babe on his knees, they exclaimed with admiration.

Paternal love gave a new impetus to his mind. In order to amass a royal dowry for his daughter, he studied the money question, about which he had previously held very primitive views. Instead of hoarding up his treasures in strong boxes, he put them out at interest. He learned all the ins and outs of speculation; he followed closely the stock-market at home and abroad. It is asserted that, struck with the advantages of the French joint-stock company, he even thought of placing brigandage on the market. He made many journeys to Europe, in the company of a Greek from Marseilles who served as interpreter. During his stay in England, he assisted at an election in, I know not what rotten borough of Yorkshire; this beautiful spectacle inspired him with profound reflections on constitutional government and its profits. He returned to Greece determined to exploit his theories and gain an income for himself. He burned a goodly number of villages in the service of the opposition; he destroyed a few others in the interests of the conservative party. When it was considered desirable to overthrow a ministry, it was only necessary to apply to him; he proved, conclusively, that the police were very corrupt and that safety could only be obtained by changing the Cabinet. But in revenge, he gave some rude lessons to the enemies of order in punishing them in whatever way they had sinned. His political talents made him so well known, that all parties held him in high esteem. His counsels, his election methods, were nearly always followed; so well that, contrary to the principle of the government representative, who wished one deputy to express the wishes of many men; he was represented, he alone, by about thirty deputies.

An intelligent Minister, the celebrated Rhalettis, suggested that a man who meddles so officiously in government affairs, might possibly, sometime, derange the machine. He undertook to bind his hands with golden cord. He made an arrangement to meet him at Carvati; between Hymettus and Pentelicus, in the country-house of a Foreign Consul. Hadgi-Stavros came, without escort and without arms. The minister and the brigand, who were old acquaintances, breakfasted together like two old friends. At the end of the meal, Rhalettis offered to him full amnesty for himself and his followers, a brevet of General of Division, title of Senator, and ten thousand hectares of forests. The Palikar hesitated some time, and at last said: "I should, perhaps, have accepted at twenty, but to-day, I am too old. I do not wish, at my age, to change my manner of living. Dusty Athens does not please me, I should go to sleep in the Senate-chamber, and if you should give me soldiers to command, I might discharge my pistols into their uniforms from force of habit. Return then, to your own affairs, and leave me to attend to mine."

Rhalettis would not own that he was beaten. He tried to enlighten the brigand as to the infamy of his life. Hadgi-Stavros laughed and said with amiability:

"My friend, the day when we shall write down our sins, which will have the longest list?"

"You think, then, that you will cheat destiny; you will die, some day or other, a violent death."

"Gracious Lord;" (Allah Kerin;) he replied in Turkish. "Neither you nor I have read the stars. But I have at least one advantage: my enemies wear a uniform and I recognize them afar off. You cannot say as much for yours. Adieu, brother."

Six months afterward, the Minister was assassinated by political enemies; the brigand still lived.

Our host did not relate to us all the exploits of his hero: the day was not long enough. He contented himself by relating the most remarkable ones. I do not believe that in any other country the rivals of Hadgi-Stavros had ever done anything more artistic than the capture of the Niebuhr. It was a steamer of the German-Lloyd which the Palikar had robbed on land, at eleven o'clock in the morning. The Niebuhr came to Constantinople; it unloaded its cargo and passengers at Calamaki, east of the Isthmus of Corinth. Four vans and two omnibusses took the passengers and merchandise to the other side of the Isthmus, to the little port of Loutraki, where another ship awaited them. It waited a long time. Hadgi-Stavros, in broad daylight, in plain view of all the world, in a flat and open country, relieved them of their merchandise, their luggage, their money and the ammunition of the soldiers who escorted the company.

"That day's work brought two hundred and fifty francs;" said Christodule to us in a tone of envy.

Much was said of Hadgi-Stavros' cruelties. His friend Christodule proved to us that he did not do wrong for pleasure. He was a sober man, who never became intoxicated, not even of blood. If it happened that he warmed, a little too much, a rich peasant's feet, it was that he might learn where the miser hid his écus. In general, he treated with kindness the prisoners for whom he hoped to receive a ransom. In the summer of '54, he descended one evening, with his band, to M. Voidi's house; he was a rich merchant from the Isle of Eubee. He found the family assembled, also an old judge of the Tribunal of Chalcis was present, taking a hand at cards with the master of the house. Hadgi-Stavros offered to play the magistrate for his liberty; he lost, and accepted with good grace." He carried off M. Voidi, his daughter and son; he left the wife that she might busy herself procuring the ransom. The day of the attack, the merchant had the gout, the daughter was ill of a fever, and the son was pale and puffy. They returned two months afterward, cured by exercise, the open air, and good entertainment. The whole family recovered health for a sum of fifty thousand francs: was it paying too high a price?

"I confess," added Christodule, "that our friend was without pity for poor payers. When a ransom was not paid on the appointed day, he promptly killed his prisoners; it was his way of protesting notes. However great may be my admiration for him, however warm the friendship between our two families, I have never pardoned him the murder of Mistra's two little daughters. They were twins of fourteen, pretty as two marble statues, both betrothed to two young men of the Leondari family. They resembled each other so exactly, that one thought one saw double and began to rub one's eyes. One morning, they went to sell cocoons; they carried between them a large basket, and they skimmed lightly over the road like two doves attached to the same car. Hadgi-Stavros took them to the mountain and wrote a letter to their mother, that he would return them for ten thousand francs, payable the end of the month. The mother was a well-to-do-widow, owner of fine mulberry groves, but poor in ready money, as we all are. She mortgaged her property, which is never easy to do, even at twenty per cent interest. It took her six weeks to gather up the sum required. When at last, she had the money, she loaded it on her mule and departed on foot for the brigand's camp. But on entering the large valley of the Taygete at the point where one finds seven fountains under a plane-tree, the mule absolutely refused to stir. Then the mother saw at the border of the path, her little girls. Their throats had been cut and their pretty heads were almost dissevered. She took the two poor creatures, put them, herself, upon the mule's back and carried them back to Mistra. She never wept; she became deranged, and died. I know that Hadgi-Stavros regretted what he had done; he believed that the widow was richer than she pretended, and that she did not wish to pay. He killed the two girls as an example. It is certain that, from that time, his outstanding debts were promptly paid and that no one dared to make him wait."

"Vile beast!" cried Giacomo, bringing his fist down with a force which made the house tremble as from an earthquake. "If ever he falls under my hand, I will serve him with a ransom of ten thousand blows of the fist, which will enable him to withdraw himself from public life."

"I," said the little Lobster with his quiet smile, "I will only ask to meet him at fifty paces from my revolver. And you, Uncle John?"

Harris whistled between his teeth a little American air, sharp as a stiletto point.

"Can I believe my ears?" added the good M. Mérinay in his flute-like voice. "Is it possible that such horrors are committed in a country like ours? I am convinced that the Society for the Moralization of Malefactors has not yet been organized in this kingdom; but while waiting for that, have you not police?"

"Certainly," replied Christodule, "fifty officers, 152 sergeants, and 1250 policemen, of whom 152 are mounted. It is the finest band of men in the kingdom after that belonging to Hadgi-Stavros."

"What astonishes me," I said in my turn, "is, that the old rascal's daughter allows him to do such things."

"She does not live with him."

"Well and good: Where is she?"

"At a boarding-school."

"In Athens?"

"You ask too much; I have known nothing of her for some time. Whoever marries her will receive a fine dowry with her."

"Yes," said Harris. "One can say as well that Calcraft's daughter is a good match."

"Who is Calcraft?"

"The Headsman of London."

At these words, Dimitri, Christodule's son, reddened to the roots of his hair. "Pardon, Monsieur," he said to John Harris, "there is a great difference between a headsman and a brigand. The business of a headsman is infamous; the profession of a brigand is honored. The government is obliged to guard the headsman of Athens in the fort Palamede or he would be assassinated; while no one wishes evil to Hadgi-Stavros, and the most respectable people in the kingdom would be proud to shake hands with him."

Harris opened his mouth to reply, when the shop bell rung. It was the servant who had entered with a young girl of fifteen or sixteen, dressed like the latest fashion-plate in the Journal des Modes. Dimitri said, as he rose from his chair: "It is Photini!"

"Messieurs," said the pastry-cook, "talk of something else, if you please. Histories of brigands are not for young girls to hear."

Christodule presented Photini to us as the daughter of one of his companions-in-arms, Colonel Jean, commanding at Nauplie. She called herself then, Photini; daughter of Jean, according to the custom of the country, where there were, properly speaking, no family names.

The young maid was ugly, as were nine-tenths of the Athenian girls. She had pretty teeth and beautiful hair, but that was all. Her thick-set body did not look well in a Parisian corset. Her feet, which were large, thick, and ill-shaped, were made for wearing Turkish slippers, and not to be compressed into the shoes of the fashionable boôt-maker, Meyer. She was as dull-looking as if an imprudent nurse had committed the fault of sitting down on her face, when an infant.

Fashion is not becoming to all women; it made the poor Photini almost ridiculous. Her flounced dress, extended over a huge crinoline, accentuated the clumsiness of her body and the awkwardness of her movements. Jewels from the Palais Royal with which she was decked seemed like exclamation points, destined to point out the imperfections of her body. You would have said that she was a stout and coarse servant-girl, masquerading in her mistress' clothes.

We were not astonished to see the daughter of a simple Colonel so extravagantly and gorgeously arrayed, come to pass Sunday at a pastry-cook's. We knew enough of the country to fully realize that dress was the incurable evil of Greek society. Country girls pierced silver pieces, strung them together and wore them upon the head on gala days. They carried their dowries on their heads. The city girls spent their money in the shops and carried their dowries on their backs.

Photini was in a boarding-school at Hétairie. It is, as you know, a school established on the model of the Legion of Honor, but regulated by rules broader and more tolerant. Usually, only daughters of soldiers were taught there, sometimes, also, brigands' heiresses.

Colonel Jean's daughter knew a little French and a little English; but her timidity did not permit of her shining in conversation. I learned later, that her family counted upon us to perfect her in these foreign tongues. Her father, having learned that Christodule boarded honorable and educated Europeans, had begged the pastry-cook to allow her to pass her Sundays with his family, and he would see that he was recompensed. This bargain pleased Christodule, and above all, his son, Dimitri. The young man, working in a servant's place, devoured her with his eyes, while the heiress never perceived it.

We had made arrangements to go, all together, to a concert. It is a fine spectacle when the Athenians give themselves up to Sunday pleasures. The entire population, in gala dress, turns out into the dusty fields, to hear waltzes and quadrilles played by a regiment band. The poor go on foot, the rich in carriages, the fashionable men on horseback. The Court would not have stayed away for an empire. After the last quadrille, each returned to his home, clothes covered with dust, but with happy hearts, and said: "We have been very well amused."

It was certain that Photini counted on showing herself at the concert, and her admirer, Dimitri, was not ashamed to appear with her; for he wore a new redingote which he had just bought at the Belle-Jardiniére. Unfortunately, it rained so steadily, that it kept us at home. To kill time, Maroula offered to let us play for bonbons; it is a favorite amusement among the middle classes. She took a glass jar from the shop, and gave to each one a handful of native bonbons, cloves, anise seed, pepper, and chicory. Then, the cards were dealt, and the first who collected nine of the same color, received three sugar plums from each of his adversaries. The Maltese, Giacomo, showed by his eagerness, that the winning was not a matter of indifference to him. Chance favored him; he made a fortune, and we saw him gulp down six or eight handfuls of bonbons which he had won from the rest of us.

I took little interest in the game, and concentrated my attention upon the curious phenomenon taking place on my left. While the glances which the young Athenian, Dimitri, cast upon Photini, were met with perfect indifference, Harris, who did not even look at her, seemed to produce a wonderful impression upon her, even to almost magnetize her. He held his cards with a nonchalant air, yawning, from time to time, with American freedom, or whistling Yankee Doodle, without respect for the company. I believe that Christodule's story had made a great impression on him, and that his thoughts were roving over the mountains in pursuit of Hadgi-Stavros. In any case, whatever his thoughts were, they were not of love. Perhaps the young girl was not thinking of it either, for Greek women nearly always have in their hearts a substratum of indifference. She looked at my friend John, as a lark looks at a mirror. She did not know him; she knew nothing of him, neither his name, his country, nor his fortune. She had not heard him speak, and even if she had heard him, she certainly was not competent to judge of his ability. She saw that he was very handsome, and that was enough. Formerly, Greeks adored beauty; it was the only one of their duties which had never had any atheists. The Greeks of to-day, despite the decadence, know how to distinguish an Apollo from a baboon. One finds in M. Fauriel's collection, a little song which may be translated thus:

"Young man, do you wish to know; young girls, would you like to learn, how love enters into our hearts? It enters by the eyes; from the eyes it descends to the heart, and in the heart it takes root!"

Decidedly, Photini knew the song; for she opened her eyes wide, so that love could enter without trouble.

The rain did not cease to fall, nor Dimitri to ogle the young girl, nor the young girl to gaze, wide-eyed, at Harris, nor Giacomo to eat bonbons, nor M. Mérinay to relate to the little Lobster, who did not listen, a chapter from Ancient History. At eight o'clock, Maroula laid the cloth for supper. Photini had Dimitri on her left, I sat at her right. She talked but little and ate nothing. At dessert, when the servant spoke of taking her home, she made a great effort and said to me in a low tone:

"Is M. Harris married?"

I took a wicked pleasure in embarrassing her a little, so I replied:

"Yes, Mademoiselle; he married the widow of the Doges of Venice."

"Is it possible; how old is she?"

"She is as old as the world, and as everlasting."

"Do not mock me; I am a poor, foolish girl, and I do not understand your European pleasantries."

"In other words, Mademoiselle, he is wedded to the sea; it is he who commands the American boat, 'The Fancy,' stationed here."

She thanked me with such a flash of radiant joy passing over her face, that her ugliness was eclipsed, and I thought she looked absolutely pretty.

III.

MARY-ANN.

The studies of my youth have developed in me one passion, to the exclusion of all others; the desire to know; or if you like the term better, call it curiosity. From the day when I embarked for Athens, my only pleasure was to learn; my only grief, ignorance. I loved science ardently, and no one, as yet, had disputed her claim in my heart. I must confess that I had little tenderness and that poetry and Hermann Schultz rarely entered the same door. I went about the world, as in a vast museum, magnifying glass in hand. I observed the pleasures and sufferings of others as emotions worthy of study, but unworthy of envy or pity. I was no more jealous of a happy household, than of two palm trees with branches interlaced by the wind; I had just as much compassion for a heart torn by love, as I had for a geranium ruined by the frost. When one has practiced vivisection, one is no longer sensitive to the quivering of the flesh. I would have been a good spectator at a combat of gladiators. Photini's love for Harris would have aroused pity in any heart but a naturalist's. The poor creature "loved at random," to quote a beautiful saying of Henry IV; and it was evident that she loved hopelessly. She was too timid to display her affection, and John was too indifferent to divine it. Even if he had noticed anything, what hope was there that he would feel any interest in an ugly Greek girl? Photini passed four days with us; the four Sundays of April. She looked at Harris from morning to night, with loving but despairing eyes; but she never found the courage to open her mouth in his presence. Harris whistled tranquilly, Dimitri growled like a young bulldog, and I smilingly looked on at this strange malady, from which my constitution had preserved me.

In the meantime, my father had written me that his affairs were not going well; that travelers were scarce; that food was dear; that our neighbors were about to emigrate; and that, if I had found a Russian princess, I had better marry her without delay. I replied that I had not, as yet, found one, unless it was the daughter of a poor Greek Colonel; that she was seriously in love, not with me, but with another; that I could by paying her a little attention become her confidant, but that I should never become her husband. Moreover, my health was good and my herbarium magnificent. My researches, hitherto restricted to the suburbs of Athens, would now become more extended. Safety was assured, the brigands had been beaten by the soldiers, and all the journals announced the dispersion of Hadgi-Stavros' band. A month or two later, I should be able to set out for Germany, and find a place which would pay enough to support the whole family.

We had read on Sunday the 28th of April, in the Siécle of Athens, of the complete defeat of "The King of the Mountains." The official reports stated that he had twenty men wounded, his camp burned, his band dispersed, and that the troops had pursued him as far as the marshes near Marathon. These reports, very agreeable to all strangers, did not appear to give much pleasure to the Greeks, and especially to our host and hostess. Christodule, for a lieutenant of troops, showed lack of enthusiasm, and Colonel Jean's daughter wept when the story of the brigand's defeat was read. Harris, who had brought in the paper, could not conceal his joy. As for me, I could roam about the country now, and I was enchanted. On the morning of the 30th, I set out with my box and my walking stick. Dimitri had awakened me at four o'clock. He was going to take orders from an English family, who had been staying for some days at the Hotel des Etrangers.

I walked down the Rue d' Hermés to the Square, Belle-Gréce, and passed through the Rue d' Eole. Passing before the Place des Canons, I saluted the small artillery of the kingdom, who slept under a shed, dreaming of the taking of Constantinople; and with four strides I was in the Rue de Patissia. The honey-flowers, which bordered either side, had begun to open their odorous blossoms. The sky, of a deep blue, whitened imperceptibly between Hymettus and Pentelicus. Before me, on the horizon, the summit of Parnassus rose like broken turrets; there was the end of my journey. I descended a path which traversed the grounds of the Countess Janthe Théotoki, occupied by the French Legation; I passed through the gardens belonging to Prince Michael Soutzo, and the School of Plato, which a President of the Areopagus had put up in a lottery some years before, and I entered the olive groves. The morning thrushes and their cousins-germain, the black-birds, flew from tree to tree, and sang joyously above my head. At the end of the wood, I traversed the immense green fields where Attic horses, short and squat, like those in the frieze at the Parthenon, consoled themselves for the dry fodder and the heating food of winter. Flocks of turtle-doves flew away at my approach, and the tufted larks mounted vertically in the sky like rockets. Once in a while, an indolent tortoise crawled across the path, dragging his house. I turned him over on his back and left him to attend to his own affairs. After two hours' walking, I entered a barren waste. Cultivation ceased; one saw upon the arid soil tufts of sickly grass, the Star of Bethlehem, or Daffodils. The sun lifted itself above the horizon, and I distinctly saw the fir-trees which grew on the side of Parnassus. The path which I had taken was not a sure guide, but I directed my steps to a group of scattered houses on the mountain side, and which was called the village of Castia.

I leaped the Céphise Eleusinien to the great scandal of the little tortoises who leaped like frogs into the water. A hundred steps further on, the path was lost in a deep and wide ravine, worn by the storms of two or three thousand winters. I supposed, reasonably enough, that the ravine ought to be the right road. I had noticed, in my former excursions, that the Greeks did not trouble themselves with making roads where streams were liable to change them. In this country, where man does not oppose the works of nature, torrents are royal roads; brooks, are department routes;

rivulets, are parish-roads. Tempests are the road-constructors, and rain is the surveyor of wide and narrow paths. I entered the ravine and walked between two river banks, which hid the plain from me. But the path had so many turns, that I should not have known in which direction I was walking, if I had not kept my back to Parnassus. The wisest course would have been to climb one bank or the other and ascertain my bearings; but the sides were perpendicular, I was weary, I was hungry; and I found the shade refreshing. I seated myself upon a bowlder of marble, I took from my box a piece of bread, some cold lamb, and a gourd of wine. I said to myself: "If I am on the right road, some one will pass and I can find out where I am."

In fact, just as I had finished lunching, and was about to stretch myself out for the rest which follows the meal of travelers or serpents, I thought I heard a horse's step. I laid my ear to the ground and heard two or three horses coming up the ravine. I buckled my box on my back, and made ready to follow them, in case they were going towards Parnassus. Five minutes afterward, I saw coming toward me, two ladies mounted upon livery-horses, and equipped like English-women on a journey. Behind them was a pedestrian, whom I had no trouble in recognizing; it was Dimitri.

You who know the world a little, you have noticed that a traveler starts out without much care for his personal appearance; but if he is about to meet ladies, though they be as old as the Dove of the Ark, he loses, at once, his indifference and looks at his dusty and travel-stained garments with a troubled eye. Before even being able to distinguish the faces of the two riders, behind their blue veils, I had looked myself over, and I was sufficiently satisfied. I wore these garments which I have on, and which are even now presentable, although that was two years ago. I have never changed the fashion of my hair; a cap, although as fine and handsome a one as this, would not have protected a traveler from the sun. I wore, instead, a large gray felt hat, which the dust could not hurt.

I took it off politely as the ladies passed me. My salutation did not appear to trouble them much. I held out my hand to Dimitri, and he told me in a few words, all that I wished to know.

"Am I upon the road to Parnassus?"

"Yes, we are going there."

"I can go with you, then?"

"Why not?"

"Who are these ladies?"

"English! Milord is resting at the hotel."

"What kind of people are they?"

"Peugh! London bankers. The old lady is Mrs. Simons, of the firm of Barley and Co.; Milord is her brother; the young lady is her daughter."

"Pretty?"

"According to taste; I like Photini's looks better."

"Are you going as far as the fortress?"

"Yes. I am engaged for a week, at ten francs a day and board. I organize and arrange their trips. I began with this one because I knew that I should meet you. But what is the matter with them now?"

The elder woman, annoyed because I was detaining her servant, had put her horse to a trot, in a passage where no one had ever dared to trot before. The other animal, filled with emulation, began to take the same gait, and if we had talked a few minutes longer, we would have been distanced. Dimitri hastened to rejoin the ladies, and I heard Mrs. Simons say to him, in English:

"Do not go away from us. I am English, and I wish to be well served. I do not pay you to chat with your friends. Who is this Greek with whom you are talking?"

"He is a German, Madame."

"Ah!—What is he doing?"

"He is searching for plants."

"He is an apothecary, then?"

"No, Madame! he is a scholar."

"Ah!—Does he know English?"

"Yes, Madame, very well."

"Ah!——"

The three "ahs!" were said in three different tones which I noticed as I would three notes of music. They indicated by very noticeable shades the progress which I had made in her esteem. She, however, addressed no word to me, and I followed them a few feet distant. Dimitri dared not speak to me; he walked ahead like a prisoner of war. All that he could do was to cast two or three looks in my direction, which seemed to say: "But these English are impertinent!" Miss Simons did not turn her head, and I was unable to decide in what her ugliness differed from Photini's. All that I could judge was, that the young English girl was large and marvelously well-formed. Her shoulders were broad, her waist was round, and supple as a reed. The little that one could see of her neck, made one think of the swans in the Zoological Gardens.

Her mother turned her head to speak to her, and I hastened forward, in hope of hearing her voice. Did I not tell you that I was extremely curious? I came up with them just in time to hear the following conversation:

"Mary-Ann!"
"Mamma!"
"I am hungry."
"Are you?"
"I am."
"Mamma, I am warm."
"Are you?"
"I am."

You believe that this truly English dialogue made me smile? Not at all, Monsieur; I was under a spell. Mary-Ann's voice had worked a charm; the truth is that as I listened, I experienced a delicious agony, and found my heart beating almost to suffocation. In all my life, I had never heard anything so young, so fresh, so silvery as that voice. The sound of a golden shower falling on my father's roof would have, truly, sounded less sweet to me. I thought to myself: "What a misfortune that the sweetest songsters among birds are necessarily the ugliest." And I feared to see her face, and yet I was consumed with eager desire to look upon it, such a strong empire has curiosity over me.

Dimitri had calculated upon reaching the inn at Calyvia at breakfast time. It was a house made of planks, loosely put together; but one could always find there a goat-skin bottle of resin wine; a bottle of rhaki; that is to say, of anise-seed cordial; some brown bread; eggs; and a regiment of venerable hens transformed by death into pullets, by virtue of metempsychosis. Unfortunately, the inn was deserted and the door closed. At this news, Mrs. Simons had a bitter quarrel with Dimitri, and as she turned around, I saw a face as sharp as the blade of a Sheffield knife, with two rows of teeth like a palisade. "I am English," she said, "and I expect to eat when I am hungry."

"Madame," Dimitri piteously replied, "you can breakfast, in half-an-hour, in the village of Castia."

I had breakfasted, and I was free to abandon myself to melancholy reflections upon Mrs. Simons' ugliness, and I murmured under my breath an aphorism in Fraugman's Latin Grammar: "Qualis mater, talis filia!"

From the inn to the village, the road was particularly detestable. It was a narrow path, between a perpendicular rock and a precipice, which made even the chamois dizzy. Mrs. Simons, before starting out on this dangerous path, where the horses could scarcely find foot-hold, asked if there was no other way. "I am English," she said, "and I was not made to roll down precipices." Dimitri began to praise the path; he assured her that there were others a hundred times worse in the kingdom. "At least," said the good lady, "take hold of the bridle. But who will lead my daughter? Go and lead my daughter's horse. Still, I must not break my own neck. Can you not lead both horses? This path is, truly, horrible. I believe that it is good enough for the Greeks, but it was not made for the English. Is it not so?" she added, turning graciously to me.

I was introduced. Regularly or not, the presentation was made. It happened under the auspices of a personage well-known in the romances of the Middle Ages, whom the poets of the XIVth century called, Danger. I bowed with all the elegance of which I was master, and replied in English:

"Madame, the path is not as bad as it appears at first sight. Your horses are sure-footed; I know them, as I have ridden them. You may have two guides, if you will permit me to lead Mademoiselle, while Dimitri leads you."

As quickly done as said; without waiting for an answer, I boldly advanced and took the bridle of Mary-Ann's horse, and as her blue veil blew back, I saw the most adorable face which has ever enchanted the sight of a German naturalist.

An eccentric poet, Aurelian Scholl, pretends that every man has in his heart a mass of eggs, in each one of which is a love. All that is needed to give life is a glance from a woman's eye. I am too much of a scholar to be ignorant of the fact that this hypothesis does not rest on sure foundations, and that it is in formal contradiction to all the revealed facts of anatomy. I ought to state, however, that Miss Simons' first glance caused a very acute agitation in the region of my heart. I experienced a sensation entirely unusual, and which bore no trace of sadness, and it seemed to me that something gave way in the osseous formation of my breast, below the bone called, sternum. At the same instant, the blood surged through my veins, and the arteries in my temples beat with such force that I could count the pulsations.

What eyes she had! I hope, for your peace of mind, that you will never meet a pair like them. They were not of unusual size, and they did not draw attention from the rest of her face. They were neither blue nor black, but of a color especially their own. It was a warm and velvety brown, which one sees only in Siberian garnets, and in certain garden flowers. I could show you a certain scabieuse, and a variety of holly-hock, nearly black, which resembles the marvelous shade of her eyes. If you have ever visited a forge at midnight, you have, doubtless, remarked the strange color which gleams from a red-hot steel plate, as it changes to a reddish brown; that too, was like her eyes. As for the charm in them, any comparison is useless. Charm is a gift with which few individuals are endowed. Mary-Ann's eyes possessed something naive and spiritual; a frank vivacity; sparkling with youth and health, and sometimes a touching languor. One read in them as in a book the knowledge of a woman and the innocence of a child; but it would have blinded one to have read the book for a long time. Her glance burned like fire, as truly as I call myself, Hermann. It would have ripened the peaches on your garden wall.

Words fail when I think that that poor simpleton, Dimitri, found her less beautiful than Photini. In truth, love is a malady which singularly stupefies its victims; I, who had never lost the use of my reason, and who judged everything with the wise indifference of a naturalist, I confess to you, that the world never held as incomparable a woman as Mary-Ann. I would like to show you her picture as it is graven in the depths of my memory. You would see what long eyelashes she had, how the eye-brows traced a beautiful arch above her eyes, how small her mouth was, how white her teeth, how rosy and transparent her little ear. I studied her beauty in the minutest details, because I possess an analytical mind and have formed habits of observation. One thing struck me especially, it was the fineness and transparency of her skin; it was more delicate than the velvety covering which envelops beautiful fruits. The color of her cheeks seemed made of that impalpable dust which adorns the wings of the butterflies. If I had not been a Doctor of Natural Sciences, I would have feared that the contact of her veil would brush off some of the luster of her beauty. I do not know whether you like pale women, or not, and I do not wish to hurt your feelings, if by chance, you have a taste for that kind of deathly looking women who have been the rage, during certain periods; but in my quality of savant, I can admire nothing without health, that joy of life. If I had become a doctor, I would have been a safe man to allow in any family, because it is certain that I should never have fallen in love with any of my patients. The sight of a pretty face, healthy and vivacious, gives me nearly as much pleasure as finding a vigorous beautiful bush, whose flowers open widely in the sunshine, and whose leaves have never been touched by butterfly or cockchafer. So that the first time that I saw Mary-Ann's face, I experienced a strong temptation to take her hand and say to her: "Mademoiselle, how happy you must be to have such good health."

I have forgotten to tell you that the lines of her face were not regular, and that her profile was not that of a statue. Phidias would, perhaps, have refused to make a bust of her; but your Pradier would have begged on his knees for sittings. I must confess, at the risk of destroying your illusions, that she had a dimple in her left cheek, but none in the right; this is contrary to all laws of symmetry. Know, moreover, that her nose was neither straight nor aquiline, but purely retroussé, as French noses are. But that this rendered her less pretty, I will deny, even upon the scaffold. She was as beautiful as Greek statues are; but was entirely different. Beauty cannot be judged by one invariable type, although Plato affirms it. It varies according to times, according to peoples, and according to culture. The Venus de Milo was considered, two thousand years ago, the most beautiful woman of the Archipelago. I do not believe that, in 1856, she would have been considered the prettiest woman in Paris. Take her to a dressmaker's in the Place Vendome, or to a milliner's in the Rue de la Paix, and in these places she would be less of a success than some other women whose features were not so classical, and whose nose was not so straight. One could admire a woman geometrically beautiful, in the days when she was only an object of art destined to please the eyes, without appealing to the mind; a bird of Paradise at whose plumage one looks, without thinking of asking it to sing. A beautiful Athenian was as well-proportioned, as white, and as cold, as the column of a temple. M. Mérinay has shown to me, in a book, that the Ionic column is only a woman, disguised. The portico of the Temple of Erechtée, at the Acropolis at Athens, rests upon four Athenian women of the century of Pericles. The women of to-day are little, winged beings, active, busy, and above all, thoughtful; created, not to hold temples on their heads, but to awaken genius, to engage in work, to animate with courage, and to light the world with the flashes of their wit. What we love in them, and what makes their beauty, is not regularity of features; it is the lively and mobile expression of sentiments, more delicate than ours; it is the radiation of thought around that fragile envelope, which does not suffice to contain it; it is the quick play of a speaking physiognomy. I am not a sculptor, but if I knew how to use the chisel and one gave me a commission to make a statue of our epoch, I swear to you that she would have a dimple in her left cheek, and a retroussé nose.

I led Mary-Ann's horse to the village of Castia. What she said to me on the way, and what I replied, left no more impression on my mind, than the flight of a swallow leaves on the air. Her voice was so sweet to listen to, that I probably did not listen to what she said. It was as if I were at the opera, where the music does not often permit one to hear the words. All the circumstances of that first interview made an ineffaceable impression on my mind. I have only to close my eyes to believe that I am still there. The April sun shone softly on my head. Above the path, and below, the resinous trees disseminated their aromatic odors through the air. The pines, the thugas, and the turpentine trees gave forth a harsh and acrid incense as Mary-Ann passed. She inhaled, with evident happiness, nature's odorous largess. Her dear little nose breathed in the fragrance; her eyes, those beautiful eyes, roved from object to object with sparkling joy. Seeing her so pretty, so lively, so happy, you would have said that a dryad had escaped from its wood. I can see now, the horse she rode; it was Psari, a white horse from Zimmerman's. Her habit was black; Mrs. Simons', which showed distinctly against the sky, was bottle-green, sufficiently eccentric to testify to her independence of taste. She also wore a black hat, of that absurd and ungraceful shape worn by men of all countries; her daughter wore the gray felt adopted by the heroines of the Fronde. Both wore chamois gloves. Mary-Ann's hand was not small, but admirably formed. I have never worn gloves, I do not like them. And you?

The village of Castia was as deserted as the inn at Calyvia. Dimitri could not understand why. We dismounted in front of the church, beside a fountain. Each went from house to house knocking at the doors; not a soul. No one at the priest's, no one at the magistrate's. The authorities of the village had moved away with the residents. Each house consisted of four walls and a roof, with two openings, one of which served as door, the other as window. Poor Dimitri forced in two or three doors, and opened five or six shutters, to assure himself that the inmates were not asleep. These incursions resulted in setting free an unfortunate cat, forgotten by its master, and which departed like a flash in the direction of the wood.

Soon, Mrs. Simons lost patience. "I am English," she said to Dimitri, "and one does not mock me with impunity. I shall complain to the Legation. What! I hire you for a trip to the mountains, and you make me travel over precipices! I order you to bring food, and you expose me to starvation! We were to breakfast at the inn! The inn is abandoned: I had the goodness to follow you, fasting, to this frightful village; and all the inhabitants have fled. All this is unnatural. I have traveled in Switzerland: Switzerland is a country of mountains; however, nothing was lacking there! and I had trout to eat, do you hear?"

Mary-Ann tried to calm her mother, but the good woman could not and would not listen. Dimitri explained to her as fully as she would permit him, that the inhabitants of the village were nearly all charcoal-burners, and that their business very often took them into the mountains. In any case, the time was not lost: it was not later than eight o'clock, and they were sure to find within ten minutes' walk an inhabited house where breakfast would be all prepared.

"What house?" demanded Mrs. Simons.

"The farm at the Convent. The monks from Pentelicus have broad lands above Castia. They raise bees there. The good old man who carries on the farm always has wine, bread, honey and fowls; he will give us our breakfast."

"He may have gone away like everyone else."

"If he is away, it will not be far. The time for the swarming is near, and he would not wish to lose his bees."

"Go and see: as for me, I have gone far enough since morning. I vow to you that I will not remount until after I have eaten."

"Madame, you need not remount," said Dimitri, patient as are all guides. "We can hitch our horses to the fountain, and we shall quickly reach the place on foot."

Mary-Ann influenced her mother to consent. She was dying to see the good old man, and his apiary. Dimitri hitched the horses to the watering trough, weighting each bridle with a huge stone. Mrs. Simons and her daughter looped up their habits and we started up a precipitous path, fit only for the goats of Castia. The green lizards which were warming themselves in the sun, discreetly retired at our approach, but each drew a piercing cry from Mrs. Simons, who had a horror of reptiles. After a quarter of an hour of these vocalizations, she had, at last, the joy of seeing an open house and a human face. It was the farmhouse and the old man.

The house was a small one made of red bricks, topped with five cupolas, almost like a mosque to the village. At a distance, it possessed a certain elegance. Comely without and coarse within, it was a sample of the Orient. One saw, in the shelter of a hill covered with thyme, a hundred straw bee-hives, placed in a line like the tents in a camp. The king of this empire, the good old man, was a small, young man of twenty-five, round and merry. All Greek monks are honored with the title of "good old man," age having nothing to do with it. He was dressed like a peasant, except his bonnet, which was black instead of red; it was by this sign that Dimitri recognized him.

The little man, seeing us running toward him, raised his arms to heaven, and appeared utterly amazed. "Here is an original," Mrs. Simons exclaimed; "what astonishes him so much? One would say that he had never seen any English people before."

Dimitri, who had run on ahead, kissed the monk's hand, and said to him with a curious mixture of respect and familiarity:

"Thy blessing, father! Wring the necks of two chickens, we will pay thee well."

"Unhappy man: why do you come here?"

"To breakfast."

"Didst thou not see that the inn was deserted?"

"I saw it so well, that I found no one at home."

"And that the village was deserted?"

"If I had met anyone, I should not have climbed up to thy house."

"Thou art then in accord with them?"

"Them? With whom?"

"The brigands."

"Are there brigands on Parnassus?"
"Since day before yesterday."
"Where are they?"
"Everywhere!"

Dimitri turned quickly toward us and said: "We have not a moment to lose. The brigands are in the mountains. Let us run for our horses. Have courage, Mesdames; and step out lively, if you please."

"This is too hard," cried Mrs. Simons. "Without having breakfasted!"

"Madame, your breakfast would cost you dear! Let us hasten, for the love of God!"

"Is this a conspiracy? You have sworn to make me die of hunger! Behold the brigands! As if there were brigands! I do not believe in brigands! All the papers state that they are disbanded! Moreover, I am English, and if anyone touched a hair of my head——!"

Mary-Ann was less confident. She leaned on my arm and asked me if I thought that we were in danger of death.

"Of death? No. Of being robbed? Yes."

"Of what importance is that? They are welcome to take all that I carry, if only they will give me my breakfast."

I learned later that the poor woman was subject to a rare malady which the vulgar call canine appetite, and our learned men know as *boulime*. When hunger assailed her, she would have given her fortune for a plate of lentils.

Dimitri and Mary-Ann each seized a hand and

dragged her to the path we had just ascended. The little monk followed her, gesticulating. I was strongly tempted to push forward; but a quick and imperative tone stopped us suddenly.

"Halt! I say!"

I raised my eyes. Two mastic bushes and arbutus-trees were on the right and left of the path. From each bush the muzzles of three or four guns protruded. A voice cried in Greek: "Seat yourselves on the ground!" This operation was exceedingly easy for me, as my knees weakened under me. But I consoled myself with the thought that Ajax, Agamemnon, and the hot-headed Achilles, if they found themselves in a like position, would not have refused the seat offered them.

The guns were lowered toward us. I expected to see them pushed out so far that their muzzles would touch each other over our heads. It was not that I was afraid; but I had never before realized the extraordinary length of Greek guns. The whole arsenal marched out into the path, showing the owner of each.

The only difference which exists between devils and brigands, is that devils are less black than one expects, and brigands more squalid than one supposes. The eight scoundrels who surrounded us were so foul, that I would have preferred to give them my money with pinchers. One could imagine that their bonnets might once have been red; but lye itself could never have found the original shade of their coats. All the rocks of the kingdom had contributed to the color of their percale skirts, and their vests bore a specimen of the different soils upon which they had reposed. Their hands, their faces, and even their mustaches were of a reddish gray like the dirt which they had on their clothes. Every animal colors itself like the house or land it inhabits: the foxes of Greenland are like the snow; lions, the color of the desert; partridges, like the ground; the Greek brigands, the color of the paths.

The chief of the little band who had taken us prisoners, was not distinguished by outward sign. Possibly his face, his hands, his clothes, were richer in dirt than those of his comrades. He bent over us from his great height, and examined us so closely, that I almost felt the touch of his gray mustache. You would have thought him a tiger who smelled his prey before devouring it. When his curiosity was satisfied, he said to Dimitri: "Empty thy pockets!" Dimitri did not make him repeat it the second time. He threw down, at his feet, a knife, a bag of tobacco, and three Mexican piastres, which made a sum of sixteen francs.

"Is that all?" demanded the brigand.

"Yes, brother."

"Thou art the servant?"

"Yes, brother."

"Take one piastre. Thou must not return to the city without money."

Dimitri began to haggle. "Thou mightest leave me two. I have two horses below; they are hired from the stable; I will have to pay for the day."

"Thou canst explain to Zimmerman that we have taken thy money."

"And if he insists on being paid even then?"

THE KING OF THE MOUNTAINS. 57

"Tell him that he is only too happy in seeing his horses again."

"He knows very well that you would not take the horses. What would you do with them in the mountains?"

"Enough! Tell me who is this tall, thin man behind thee?"

I answered for myself: "An honest German whose spoils will not enrich you."

"Thou speakest Greek; well. Empty thy pockets!"

I placed on the ground twenty francs, my tobacco, my pipe and my handkerchief.

"What is that?"

"A handkerchief."

"What for?"

"To wipe my nose."

"Why didst thou tell me that thou wert poor? Only lords wipe their noses with handkerchiefs. Take off the box which thou carriest on thy back. That is well! Now open it."

My box contained some plants, a book, a knife, a small packet of arsenic, an almost empty gourd of wine, and the remains of my breakfast which brought a gleam of covetousness to Mrs. Simons' eyes. I had the impudence to offer them to her before my property changed hands. She snatched them greedily and began to devour the bread and meat. To my great astonishment, this gluttonous act disgusted the thieves, who murmured among themselves the word *heretic!* The monk made a half-dozen signs of the cross, according to the rite of the Greek church.

"Thou probably hast a watch," said the brigand to me, "put it with the other things."

I took off my silver watch, an heirloom, which weighed about four ounces. The rascals passed it from hand to hand and found it very beautiful. I hoped that admiration, which softens men's feelings, would dispose them to restore to me something of my belongings, and I begged the Chief to give me my tin box. He rudely told me to keep silent. "At least," I persisted, "give back my two écus so that I can return to the city." He replied with a sardonic grin: "Thou wilt have no use for them."

Mrs. Simons' turn had come. Before putting her hand into her pocket, she addressed our captors in the tongue of her fathers. English is one of the rare languages which one can speak with one's mouth full. "Reflect well upon what you are doing," she said in a menacing tone. "I am an Englishwoman, and English subjects are sacred in every country in the world. What you take from me will serve you little, and cost you dear. England will avenge me, and you will be hung, at the very least. Now, if you wish my money, you have only to speak; but it will burn your fingers; it is English money!"

"What does she say?" asked the leader of the brigands.

Dimitri answered: "She says she is English."

"So much the better; all the English are rich. Tell her to shell out!"

The poor woman emptied her pocket; her purse contained a dozen sovereigns. As her watch was not in sight, and as they did not search us, she kept that. The kindness of these thieves left her her handkerchief.

Mary-Ann threw down her watch and a string of charms against the evil eye. She took off, with mutinous grace, a shagreen-leather bag, which she wore slung on her shoulder. The bandit opened it with all the importance of a custom-house officer. He took out an English dressing-case, a bottle of English smelling-salts, a box of English Menthol pastilles and a hundred and several odd francs of English money.

"Now," said the enraged beauty, "you can let us go; we have nothing more for you."

One of the men indicated to her by a menacing gesture, that the interview was not yet over. The leader of the band knelt down before their spoils, called the monk, counted the money in his presence and gave to him a sum of forty-five francs. Mrs. Simons nudged me. "Do you see?" she whispered; "the monk and Dimitri have betrayed us into their hands; the bandits have divided with them!"

"No, Madame," I replied, "Dimitri has received only a fraction of what was taken from him. It is customary everywhere. On the borders of the Rhine, when a traveler is ruined at roulette, the banker gives him enough to return home."

"But the monk?"

"He has only received the tithe of the spoils, according to custom from time immemorial. Do not reproach him, but rather be grateful to him in his wish to save us, when his convent would have benefited by our capture."

This conversation was interrupted by Dimitri's departure. They had told him that he was free. "Wait for me," I said to him, "we will return together." He sadly shook his head and answered in English, so that the ladies could understand:

"You are prisoners for a time, and you will not see Athens again until you have paid a ransom. I am going to inform milord. Have the ladies any message to send to him?"

"Tell him," cried Mrs. Simons, "that he must hurry to the Ambassador, that he must go to Piraeus to find the Admiral, that he must complain at the Foreign Office, and he must surely write to Lord Palmerston! That we must be rescued from here by force of arms, if necessary, or by political authority; but that I will not hear of paying one penny for my liberty."

"And I," I said with less anger, "I pray thee to tell my friends in whose hands thou hast left me. If it is necessary to have a few hundred drachmas to ransom a poor devil of a naturalist, they will furnish them without doubt. The lords of the road will not put a very high price on me. I wish whilst thou art still here, that thou wouldst ask them the price."

"Useless, my dear M. Hermann, they do not fix the ransom."

"Who, then?"

"Their chief, Hadgi-Stavros."

IV.

HADGI-STAVROS.

Dimitri descended to Athens; the monk went back to his bees; our new masters pushed us into the path which led to the camp of their king. Mrs. Simons rebelled and refused to stir a step. The brigands threatened to carry her in their arms; she declared that she would not let them carry her. But her daughter talked her into a more tractable frame of mind, telling that she would find the table spread and that she would be invited to breakfast by Hadgi-Stavros. Mary-Ann was more surprised than frightened. The followers who had come to arrest us, had acted with a certain courtesy; they had not searched us, and they had kept their hands from their prisoners. Instead of turning our pockets wrong side out, they had asked us to put down our money and valuables ourselves; they made no remark about the ladies' ear-rings and they did not even ask them to take off their gloves. We were far, it seemed, from those highwaymen in Spain and Italy who cut off a finger to get a ring and who tear out an ear-ring to possess themselves of a diamond or pearl. All these misfortunes were reduced to the payment of a ransom; yet was it not probable that we might be delivered without it? How could one imagine that Hadgi-Stavros would be able to hold us with impunity, at five leagues from the capital, from the court, from the Greek army, from her Britannic Majesty's battalion, at an English station. Thus reasoned Mary-Ann. As for me—I, involuntarily, thought of those two little daughters whom Mistra went to seek, and I was sad. I feared that Mrs. Simons, in her obstinate patriotism, only exposed her daughter to some great danger, and I promised myself that I would enlighten her as to her position. We walked in a narrow path, single file, separated from each other by our disagreeable companions. The journey seemed to me to be interminable, and I asked more than ten times, if we would not soon be there. The road was frightful; in the crevices of the bare rock an oak sapling struggled for life, or a thorny bush scratched our legs. The victorious bandits manifested no joy, and their triumphal march resembled a funeral parade. They silently smoked cigarettes as large as one's finger.

They did not speak; one, only, now and then hummed a sort of tune. Those people are as lugubrious as a ruin.

About eleven o'clock, a fierce barking announced the neighborhood of the camp. Ten or a dozen enormous dogs rushed out and hurled themselves upon us, showing all their teeth. Our captors drove them back with stones, and after a quarter of an hour of hostilities, peace was declared. These inhospitable monsters were the advance sentinels of the King of the Mountains. They scent the soldiers as a contrabandist's dog scents a custom-house officer. But that is not all, and their zeal is so great, that they, occasionally, devoured an inoffensive shepherd, a lost traveler, or even one of Hadgi-Stavros' band. The King kept them, as the old

Sultans kept their Janissaries, with the perpetual fear of falling a victim to them.

The King's camp was a plateau of seven or eight hundred metres in extent. I searched everywhere for our captors' tents. The brigands were not sybarites, and they slept under the sky on the 30th of April. I saw neither heaps of spoils nor a display of treasures, nothing which one would hope to find at the headquarters of a band of brigands. Hadgi-Stavros took upon himself the sale of the plunder; each man received his pay in silver and used it according to his fancy. Some put their money into commerce, others invested in mortgages on houses in Athens, while others bought land in their villages; no one squandered the proceeds of theft. Our arrival interrupted the morning meal of twenty-five or thirty men, who hastened to meet us, bread and cheese in hand. The Chief furnished his band with food: the men received, every day, a ration of bread, oil, wine, cheese, caviare, piment (wine mixed with honey and spices), bitter olives, and meat when their religion permitted. Gourmands who wish for mallows and other green food, can pick these dainties on the mountains. Brigands, as some other classes of people, rarely light a fire for their repasts; they eat their food cold, and their vegetables uncooked. I noticed that everyone was religiously observing the law of abstinence. We were on the eve of the celebration of the Ascension, and these good people, of whom the most innocent had at least the life of one man on his conscience, would not touch a mouthful of meat. Holding up two Englishwomen, at the point of a musket, seemed an insignificant sin; Mrs. Simons had very greatly sinned in eating the cold meat, the Wednesday before Ascension. The men who had escorted us, satisfied the curiosity of their comrades. They were overwhelmed with questions and they answered them all. They put down in a pile, the booty they had secured, and my silver watch scored yet another success, which added to my pride. Mary-Ann's little gold watch was less noticed. In that first interview, public attention fell upon my watch, and it reflected a little on me. In the eyes of these simple men, the owner of such an imposing piece of silver could be no less than a lord.

The bandits' curiosity was annoying, but not insolent. They did not treat us harshly. They knew that we were in their hands and that we would be exchanged, sooner or later, for a certain number of gold pieces; but they did not think that they ought to avail themselves of that circumstance to maltreat us, or show a lack of respect. Good sense, that imperishable spirit of the Greeks, told them that we represented a different race, and one, to a certain degree, superior. Victorious barbarians render a secret homage to a conquered civilized people. Many of these men saw for the first time, the European dress. These walked around us, as the inhabitants of the new world around Columbus' Spaniards. They furtively felt my coat, to see of what material it was made. They would have been happy to have examined the articles of my clothing, one by one. Perhaps, even, they would have liked to break me in two or three pieces, in order to study the inner mechanism of a lord, but I am sure that they would have done it with profuse excuses, and not without asking pardon for the liberty.

Mrs. Simons soon lost patience; she did not like to be examined so closely by these cheese-eaters, who offered her no breakfast. No one likes to be made a spectacle of. The role of "living curiosity" very much displeased the good woman, although she had filled it advantageously in all countries of the globe. As for Mary-Ann, she was overcome with fatigue. A ride of six hours, hunger, emotion, surprise, had worn out this delicate creature. Imagine this young girl, brought up delicately, accustomed to walk on carpets, or upon the velvety turf of parks. Her shoes were already nearly off her feet, worn out by the roughness of the path, and the bushes had torn her dress. Only the evening before she had taken tea in the parlors of the English Legation, while looking over the beautiful albums belonging to Mr. Wyse. She now found herself transported into a frightful country, in the midst of a crowd of savages, and she had not the consolation of saying: "It is a dream!" because she was neither in bed, nor even seated, but standing, in great despair, on her two weary little feet.

A band now surrounded us, which rendered our position intolerable. It was not a band of thieves; it was worse. The Greeks carry upon their persons a whole menagerie of little animals, agile, capricious, not seizable, who cling to them night and day, give them occupation even when asleep, and by their jumps and their stings, accelerate the action of the mind, and the circulation of the blood. The fleas of the brigands, of which I can show some specimens in my Entomological collection, are very much larger, stronger and more agile than their city cousins; the open country air possesses virtue so powerful! I soon perceived that they were not content with their lot, and that they found more to their taste, the fine skin of a young German than the tough hide of their masters. An emigrating army settled upon me. I felt, at first, an uneasy sensation around the ankles: it was the declaration of war. Two minutes later, an advance guard threw itself upon the calf of my right leg; it reached my knee. I was out-flanked, and all resistance became useless. If I had been alone, I might have been more successful in the combat.

I dared neither complain nor defend myself; I heroically hid my sorrows and did not raise my eyes.

At last, at the end of my patience, and determined to escape, by flight, from the pests, I demanded to be taken before the King. This recalled our guides to their duty. They asked the whereabouts of Hadgi-Stavros. The reply was that he was at work in his offices.

"At last," said Mrs. Simons, "I can seat myself in an easy chair."

She took my arm, offered hers to her daughter, and walked, with a deliberate step, in the direction in which the crowd conducted us. The offices were not far from the camp, and we reached them in five minutes.

The offices of the King resembled other offices, as the bandits' camp was like to other camps. There

THE KING OF THE MOUNTAINS. 67

were neither tables, chairs nor furniture of any sort. Hadgi-Stavros was seated, tailor-fashion, upon a square of carpet, under the shade of a fir tree. Four secretaries and two servants sat around him.

A young boy of sixteen or eighteen, was incessantly occupied in filling, lighting and cleaning his master's chibouk. He wore at his belt a tobacco bag, embroidered with gold and fine pearls, and a pair of silver tongs, used for taking out coals. Another servant passed his days preparing cups of coffee, glasses of water and syrup, destined for the royal mouth.

The secretaries, seated on the bare rock, wrote with cut reeds, upon their knees. Each of them had a long copper box containing reeds, a knife and an inkstand. Some tin cylinders, like those in which soldiers keep their papers, served as a place of safety for their archives. The paper was not poor, for the reason that each sheet bore in capitals the word "Bath."

The King was an old man, marvelously well-preserved, straight, thin, supple as a steel spring, clean and shining as a new sword. His long, white mustaches hung over the chin, like two marble stalactites. The rest of his face was scrupulously shaved, the cranium bare as far as the occiput, where a great mass of white hair flowed down from under his bonnet. The expression of his face was calm and reflective. A pair of small, clear blue eyes, and a square-cut chin denoted an inflexible will. His face was long, and the many long wrinkles added to its length. Every fold in his forehead seemed to break in the middle and diverge toward the meeting of his eyebrows; two wide and deep furrows descended to the corners of the lips, as if the weight of the mustaches dragged down the muscles of the face. I have seen a great number of septuagenarians, I have even dissected one who would have attained a hundred, if the diligence from Osnabruck had not passed over his body; but I never remembered having seen an old man fresher and more robust than Hadgi-Stavros.

He wore the dress of Tino and all the islands of the Archipelago. His red bonnet formed a large fold around his forehead. He wore a black vest, heavily embroidered with black silk, immense blue trousers which must have taken twenty metres of cotton stuff, and large boots of Russia leather, solid yet supple. The only richness about his costume, was a belt decked with gold and precious stones, worth two or three thousand francs. Thrust in it, was a purse of embroidered cashmere, a Damascus blade in a silver sheath, a long pistol, mounted with gold and rubies, and a ramrod, similarly decorated.

Immovable in the midst of his secretaries, the King moved only his lips and his fingers; his lips to dictate his letters, his fingers to tell off the beads of his rosary. It was one of those beautiful milk-white amber rosaries which serve, not only to mark the number of prayers, but to amuse the solemn idleness of the Turks.

He raised his head at our approach, divined, by a glance, what had brought us to him, and said, with a gravity, not at all ironical; "You are very welcome! Be seated."

"Monsieur," cried Mrs. Simons, "I am English, and——"

He interrupted the discourse: "All in good time," he said; "I am occupied." He spoke in Greek and Mrs. Simons understood only English, but the King's face was so expressive, that the good woman easily comprehended what he meant without the aid of an interpreter. We sat down on the ground. Fifteen or twenty brigands crouched around us, and the King, who had no secrets to hide, dictated family letters as well as those pertaining to business. The leader of the band which had arrested us, went to him and whispered in his ear. He haughtily answered: "What of that? I am doing nothing wrong, and the whole world is welcome to hear me. Go, seat thyself; Thou, Spiro, write: it is to my daughter."

After he had vigorously blown his nose, he dictated in a grave, yet sweet voice:

"My Dear Child:
"The preceptress of the school writes to me that thy health is much improved and that the severe cold with which thou wast troubled, has left thee with the cold winter weather. But she is not pleased with thy lack of application, and complains that thou hast done nothing with thy studies during the month of April. Mme. Mavros writes that thou hast become distrait, and that thou sittest with thy elbow on thy book, thy eyes looking at nothing, as if thou wert thinking of something else. I know that it is unnecessary to tell thee to work assiduously. Follow the example of my life. If I had taken it easy, as many do, I should never have reached the position which I occupy in society. I wish to have thee worthy of me, that is why

I make great sacrifices for thy education. Thou knowest that I have never refused thee the masters nor the books for which thou hast asked; but my money must profit by it. The set of 'Walter Scott,' has arrived at Piraeus, also the 'Robinson,' and all the other English books thou hast said that thou didst wish to read; have our friends in the Rue d' Hèrmes get them from the Custom-House for thee. Thou wilt receive, at the same time, the bracelet which thou desirest, and that steel machine for puffing out thy skirts. If the piano from Vienna is not as good as thou toldest me, and it seems necessary that thou shouldst have another, thou shalt have it. I shall do one or two villages, after the sales of the harvest, and the Devil will be against me, if I cannot find enough money for a pretty piano. I think, as thou dost, that thou must learn music. Use thy Sundays in the way I have told thee, and profit by the kindness of our friends. Thou must learn to speak French, English, and above all, German. Because, thou art not to live forever in this ridiculous country, and I would rather see thee dead than married to a Greek. Daughter of a King, thou shouldst, by right, marry a Prince. I do not mean, a prince of smugglers, like all our Fanariot families, who pride themselves on their descent from Oriental emperors, and whom I would not have for servants; but a Prince, reigning and crowned. One can find some very good ones in Germany, and my fortune will enable me to choose one of them. If these Germans come to reign in this country, I do not see why thou canst not reign there, in thy turn. Make haste, then, to learn the language, and tell me in thy next letter of the progress thou hast made. My child, I embrace thee tenderly, and I send thee, with thy quarter's allowance, my paternal blessing."

Mrs. Simons leaned toward me and whispered: "Is he dictating our sentence to his brigands?"

THE KING OF THE MOUNTAINS. 71

I replied: "No, Madame; he is writing to his daughter."

"Concerning our capture?"

"Concerning a piano, a crinoline, and Walter Scott."

"That takes a long time. Will he invite us to breakfast?"

"There comes a servant with refreshments."

The King's coffee-bearer came to us, bringing three cups of coffee, a box of rahat-loukoum, and a pot of preserves. Mrs. Simons and her daughter rejected the beverage with disgust, because it was made like Turkish coffee, and was like thickened milk. I emptied my cup like a veritable gourmand of the Orient. The pot of sweets was a rose sorbet, and received only a small share of our attention, as we were forced to eat it with one spoon. Delicate eaters are unfortunate when in this country of primitive simplicity. But the rahat-loukoum, cut in pieces, pleased the palates of the ladies, without shocking too much, their ordinary tastes. They took in their beautiful fingers that perfumed jellied paste, and emptied the box, while the King dictated the following letter:

"Messrs. Barley and Company,
    "31 Cavendish Square,
        "London.

"I see by your honored letter of the 5th of April and the current account which accompanies it, that I have, at the present time, 22,750 livres sterling, to my credit. Please place these funds, half in English three per cents, half in shares of the company, before the coupons are cut. Sell my shares of the Royal Britannic Bank; it is an institution in which I have no longer any confidence. Take for me, in exchange, all in Bank of London. If you can get 15,000 livres for my house in the Strand (it was valued at that in 1852), you may buy for me, in the Vieille-Montagne, an equal amount. Send to the firm, Rhalli Brothers, 100 guineas; it is my subscription for the Hellenic School at Liverpool. I have seriously pondered the proposition which you have done me the honor to submit to me, and, after many reflections, I have decided to persist in my line of conduct and transact business strictly on a cash basis. Purchases in future are of a speculative character, which ought to prevent any good father of a family from dealing in them. I am assured that you would not expose my capital to danger, and would use it with a prudence which has always characterized your house; but even where the benefit of which you write, seems sure, I experience, I must confess it, a certain repugnance to leaving to my heirs a fortune augmented by gambling. Accept, etc.,

"Hadgi-Stavros,
"Proprietor."

"Is it about us?" Mary-Ann whispered.

"Not yet, Mademoiselle, His Majesty is investing in stocks."

"In stocks! Here? I thought that was only done at home."

"Is Monsieur, your father, associated with a banking establishment?"

"Yes; with the firm of Barley & Co."

"Are there two bankers of the same name in London?"

"Not that I am aware of."

"Have you ever heard that the firm transacted business with the Orient?"

"Certainly, all over the world."

"And do you live in Cavendish Square?"

"No, the offices are there. Our house is in Piccadilly."

"Thank you, Mademoiselle. Allow me to listen to the next. This old man's correspondence is very interesting."

The King dictated, without stopping, a long report of the shares of his band. This curious document was addressed to M. Georges Micrommati, Officer of Ordinance, at the Palaces, that he might read it in the General Assembly to those interested.

"Account rendered of the operations of the National Company by the King of the Mountains.

Receipts and Expenditures, 1855-56.

Sirs: Camp of the King, April 30, '56.

The agent whom you have honored with your confidence, to-day, for the fourteenth time, submits for your approval the report of the year's transactions. Since the day when the constitutional act of our society was signed in the office of Master Tsappas, Royal Notary of Athens, never has our enterprise encountered more obstacles, never has the progress of our labors been embarrassd by more serious difficulties. It is in the presence of a strange occupation, under the eyes of two armies, if not hostile, at least ill-disposed, that the regular practice of an eminently national institution must be carried on. Piraeus is occupied by the military; the Turkish frontier is watched with a zealousness without precedent in history, and this restricts our activity to a very narrow circle, and confines our zeal to impassable limits. Within these narrow boundaries, our resources are still more reduced by the general penury, the scarcity of money, and the small crops. The olive trees have not yielded as they promised; the cereal harvests have been small, and the vines are not yet rid of the oïdium. In these circumstances it has been difficult to profit by the tolerance of the authorities and the kindness of a friendly government. Our enterprise is so identified with the interests of the country, that it can flourish only in the general prosperity, and so repulse the counterstrokes of all public calamities; for from those who have nothing, one can take nothing, or little of anything.

The strangers traveling in this country, whose curiosity is so useful to the kingdom and to us, have become rare. English tourists, who, formerly, composed an important branch of our revenue, are totally lacking. Two young Americans, stopped upon the road to Pentelicus, lost us their ransom. The French and English papers had inspired them with a spirit of defiance, and they escaped from our hands, at a time when their capture would have been most useful.

And now, gentlemen, this is our record, a report of our society which has resisted the fatal crisis better than agriculture, industries and commerce. Your funds, confided to my keeping, have been made profitable, not as much so as I could wish, but better than any one could hope for. I will say no more; I leave the figures to speak for themselves. Arithmetic is more eloquent than Demosthenes.

The society capital, limited at first to the modest sum of 50,000 francs, has increased to 120,000 by three successive issuings of bonds of 500 francs.

Our gross receipts, from May 1, 1855, to April 30, 1856, are 261,482 francs.

Expenses as follows:

Tithes paid to churches and monasteries.... 26,148
Interest on capital of the legal tax of 10 per
    cent per 100......................... 12,000
                                              38,148

Report.

Pay and board for 80 men at 650 francs per capita	52,000
Material, arms, etc.	7,056
Repairing the road to Thebes, which had become impassable and where there were no travelers to hold up	2,540
Expense of watching the highways	5,835
Rent for office	3
Subsidizing some journalists	11,900
Rewards to various employes of the judicial and administrative orders	18,000
Total	135,482
If this sum is deducted from the gross receipts, there are left, net	126,000

According to the statutes, the above is apportioned as follows:

Reserve funds in the Bank of Athens	6,000
Share belonging to Agent	40,000
Share-holders' part	80,000

333 francs, 33 c. per share.

Add to the 333 francs, 33 c., 50 francs interest and 25 francs in reserve funds, and you will have a total of 408 francs, 33 c. per share. Your money is then drawing nearly 82 per cent.

Such are the results, gentlemen, of the last campaign. Judge what the future will be, when our country and our operations shall be free from the foreign power which presses so heavily."

The King dictated this without consulting any notes, without hesitating about a figure and without stopping to choose words. I would never have believed that an old man of his age could have possessed so remarkable a memory. He appended his seal to the three letters;

it was his way of signing. He read easily, but he had never found time to learn to write. Charlemagne and Alfred the Great were, it is said, in the same predicament.

While the Under-Secretaries of State were transcribing the letters for the day in order to place them in the archives, he gave audience to subaltern officers who had returned with their detachments, from the day's duty. Each man seated himself in front of him, saluted him by laying his right hand on his heart and making his report in a few words. I swear to you that Saint-Louis, under his oak, inspired no greater reverence among the people of Vincennes.

The first who presented himself was a small man, with a bad face; a fine sample for the Court of Assizes. It was an islander from Corfu, persecuted as an incendiary: he had been well brought up, and his talents had advanced him. But his chief and his soldiers held him in no great esteem. He was suspected of keeping for his own profit a part of the spoils. Now the King was unreasonable on the subject of probity. When he found a man in fault, he ignominiously thrust him out and ironically said to him: "Go and make a magistrate of thyself!"

Hadgi-Stavros asked the man from Corfu: "What hast thou done?"

"I have just come, with my fifteen men, from the ravine of Cirondelles, upon the road to Thebes. I met a detachment of soldiers; twenty-five men."

"Where are their guns?"

"I left them. They were percussion muskets, which would not serve us on account of lack of caps."

"Good! Then?"

"It was market-day; I stopped the passers-by."

"How many?"

"One hundred and forty-two persons."

"And thou hast brought——?"

"About a thousand francs," naming the sum.

"Seven francs per head! It is small!"

"It is good. They were peasants."

"They had not, then, sold their goods?"

"Some had sold, others bought."

The man opened a heavy sack which he carried under his arm; he spread out the contents before the secretaries, who began to count the amount. The receipts were from thirty to forty Mexican piastres, some handfuls of Austrian zwanzigs and an enormous quantity of copper coins. Some crumpled papers were among the money. They were bank notes of ten francs each.

"Thou hast no jewels?" asked the King.

"No!"

"Were there no women, then?"

"I found nothing worth bringing away."

"What is that on thy finger?"

"A ring."

"Gold?"

"Or copper; I do not know which."

"Where didst thou get it?"

"I bought it two months ago."

"If thou hadst bought it, thou wouldst know whether it was gold or copper. Give it to me."

The man took it off with bad grace. The ring was immediately locked up in a small coffer full of jewels.

"I pardon thee!" said the King, "because of thy bad education. The people of thy country disgrace theft by mixing knavery with it. If I had only Ionians in my band, I would be obliged to place turnstiles in the roads as they do at the Exposition in London, so that I might count the visitors and the money. The next!"

He, who came forward now, was a tall young man, well-proportioned, and with a most pleasing face. His round eyes beamed forth rectitude and good-nature. His lips, half-opened with a pleasant smile, showed a magnificent set of teeth; I was greatly taken with him, and I said to myself that if he had been led astray by evil associations, he must surely return, some day, to the right path. My face must have pleased him, for he saluted me very politely, before seating himself in front of the King.

Hadgi-Stavros said to him: "What hast thou done, Vasile?"

"I reached Pigadia, yesterday evening, with my six men; it is the village of the Senator Zimbellis."

"Well!"

"Zimbellis was absent, as usual; but his relatives, his farmers, and his tenants were all at home, and in bed."

"Well!"

"I entered an inn; I awakened the landlord; I bought

twenty-five bundles of straw, and for payment I killed him."

"Well!"

"We carried the straw to the houses, and spread it around; the houses are of wood or osier, and we set fire to seven places at once. The matches were good; the wind from the north; everything went."

"Well!"

"We retired quietly to the wells. The whole village awakened and rushed out, shouting. The men came running with their leather buckets to get water. We drowned four whom we did not know; the others escaped."

"Well!"

"We returned to the village. There was no one, only an infant forgotten by his parents, and who cried like a little raven fallen from its nest. I threw him into a burning house, and he cried no more."

"Well!"

"Then we took fire-brands, and placed them around the olive trees. The thing was well-executed. We then started for the camp; we supped and slept about half-way here, and we arrived at nine o'clock, in prime condition without even a burn."

"Good! The Senator Zimbellis will not discourse against us again! The next!"

Vasile withdrew, saluting me as he passed, as politely as the first time; but I did not return his bow.

He was soon replaced by the great devil who had taken us. By a singular caprice of chance, the first author of the drama in which I was called to play a part, was named Sophocles. At the moment when he began his report, I felt the blood congeal in my veins. I supplicated Mrs. Simons not to risk an imprudent word. She replied, that she was English, and that she knew how to behave herself. The King asked us to be silent, and allow the man to speak.

He first spread out the booty which he had taken from us; then he drew from his belt forty Austrian ducats, which made a sum of four hundred and seventy francs, at the rate of 11 francs-15c.

"The ducats," he said, "came from the village of Castia; the rest was taken from these nobles. Thou didst tell me to scour the boundaries, I began with the village."

"Thou hast not done well," replied the King. "The people of Castia are our neighbors, they must not be molested. How can we live in safety, if we have enemies at our door? Moreover, they were brave people who have given us aid when occasion demanded."

"Oh! I took nothing from the charcoal burners. They disappeared into the woods, without giving me time to speak to them. But the padre had the gout; I found him at home."

"What didst thou say to him?"

"I asked him for his money; he insisted that he had none. I shut him up in a sack with his cat; and I do not know what the cat did, but he began to cry out that his treasure was behind the house, under a huge stone."

"Thou wert wrong. The padre will incite all the village against us."

"Oh! no! In leaving him, I forgot to open the sack, and the cat ought to have fixed him by this time."

"All in good time:——But listen to me well, all of you: I do not wish anyone to trouble our neighbors. Thou mayst retire."

Our examination now began. Hadgi-Stavros, instead of having us come to him, gravely rose, came and seated himself on the ground in front of us. This mark of deference to us seemed a favorable augury. Mrs. Simons prepared to question him herself. As for me, perceiving too well what she was capable of saying, and knowing the intemperance of her tongue, I offered my services to the King, as interpreter. He thanked me coldly, and called the Corfuan, who knew English.

"Madame," the King said to Mrs. Simons, "you seem to be in great anger. Have you any complaints to make of the men who brought you here?"

"It is a horror!" she cried. "Your rascals have arrested, dragged me through the dirt, despoiled me, worn me out, and starved me."

"Will you accept my excuses? I am forced to employ men without education. Believe me, my dear Madame, it is not by my orders they have acted thus. You are English?"

"An Englishwoman from London."

"I have been to London; I know and esteem the English. I know that they have good appetites, and you noticed that I was moved to offer you refreshments. I know that ladies of your country do not like to run over rocks, and I regret that you were not allowed to walk your own gait. I know that people of your nation carry, while traveling, only such things as are necessary, and I have not yet pardoned Sophocles for having robbed you, above all, if you are a person of distinction."

"I belong to the best society of London!"

"Deign to take back your money. You are rich?"

"Assuredly."

"This traveling-case is yours, is it not?"

"It is my daughter's."

"Take, also, all that belongs to your daughter. You are very rich?"

"Very rich."

"Do these things belong to Monsieur, your son?"

"Monsieur is not my son; he is a German. Since I am English how could I have a German son?"

"That is true. Have you twenty thousand francs income?"

"More."

"A carpet for these ladies! Are you rich enough to have thirty thousand francs income?"

"We have more than that."

"Sophocles is a villain whom I shall chastise. Logothète, tell them to prepare dinner for these ladies. May it be possible, Madame, that you are a millionaire?"

"I am that."

"And I—I am annoyed at the way in which you have

been treated. You have, without doubt, fine friends in Athens?"

"I know the English Minister."

"Oh! Madame! You also know some merchants, some bankers?"

"My brother, who is at Athens, knows many bankers in the city."

"I am delighted. Sophocles, come here. Ask pardon of these ladies."

Sophocles muttered some words between his teeth, I know not what excuses. The King replied:

"These ladies are Englishwomen of distinction; they are worth a million or more; they have been received by the English Ambassador; their brother, who is in Athens, knows all the bankers in the city."

"That is right!" cried Mrs. Simons. The King continued:

"Thou shouldst have treated these ladies with all the regard due their fortune."

"Good!" Mrs. Simons cried.

"Have conducted them here carefully."

"For what purpose?" murmured Mary-Ann.

"And abstained from touching their baggage. When one has the honor of meeting, in the mountains, two persons of the rank of these ladies, one should salute them with respect, one should bring them to the camp with deference, one should guard them circumspectly, and one should offer them politely every necessary thing in life, until their brother or their ambassador sends us a ransom of a hundred thousand francs."

Poor Mrs. Simons! dear Mary-Ann! Neither expected this termination. As for me, I was not surprised. I knew with what a crafty knave we had to do. I took up the word, and I said to him fiercely: "Thou canst keep what thy men have taken from me, because it is all that thou wilt get from me. I am poor, my father has nothing, my brothers often eat dry bread. I know neither bankers nor ambassadors, and if thou keepest me with the hope of a ransom, thou wilt reap no reward. I swear it to thee!"

A murmur of incredulity was heard, but the King appeared to believe me.

"If that is true," he said to me, "I will not keep you. I will send you back to the city. Madame will give you a letter for Monsieur, her brother, and you may even leave to-day. If, however, you need to remain a day or two in the mountains, I will offer my hospitality to you; because I suppose that you have not come as far as this, with this large box, in order to look over the country."

This little speech gave me a profound feeling of relief. I looked around with satisfaction. The King, his secretaries, and his soldiers seemed less terrible; the surrounding rocks more picturesque, since I viewed them with the eye of a guest and not as a prisoner. The desire I had experienced to see Athens suddenly subsided, and I decided to pass two or three days in the mountains. I felt that my counsels would not be useless to Mary-Ann's mother. The good woman was in a state of excitement which might urge her to do something rash. If, perchance, she determined to refuse to pay the ransom! Before England could come to her aid, she would have ample time to draw dire calamity upon her charming head. I must not leave her until I had an opportunity to relate the history of Mistra's little daughters. Shall I say more? You know my passion for botany. The flora of Parnassus is very enticing at the end of April. One can find in the mountains five or six plants as rare as they are celebrated. One especially: Boryana variabilis, discovered and named by M. Bory de Saint-Vincent. Should I leave such a lacuna and present my herbarium to the Museum of Hamburg, without the boryana variabilis?"

I replied to the King: "I accept thy hospitality, but on one condition."

"What is it?"

"That thou wilt return my box."

"Oh well! so be it: and the condition?"

"That is it."

"Will you tell me of what use it is to you?"

"To hold the plants which I pick."

"And why do you search for plants? To sell them?"

"Nonsense! I am not a merchant, I am a savant."

He held out his hand to me and said with visible joy: "I am charmed. Science is a beautiful thing. Our ancestors were wise men. Our grand-children will be, perhaps. As for us, time is lacking. Savants are much esteemed in your country?"

"Greatly."

"One gives them rank?"

"Sometimes."

"One pays them well?"

"Enough!"

"One attaches a little ribbon to their coat?"

"Occasionally!"

"Is it true that cities dispute as to which they belong?"

"It is true in Germany!"

"And one looks upon their death as a public calamity?"

"Assuredly!"

"What you tell me gives me great pleasure. Then you have no complaints to make of your fellow-citizens?"

"Very much to the contrary. It is through their liberality that I was enabled to come to Greece."

"You travel at their expense?"

"Yes."

"You are well-educated?"

"I am a doctor."

"It is the highest grade in science?"

"No."

"And how many doctors are there in the city in which you live?"

"I do not know exactly, but not as many doctors in Hamburg, as generals in Athens."

"Oh! oh! I would not deprive your country of a man so rare. You shall return to Hamburg, Monsieur, doctor; what would they say down below if they knew that you were a prisoner up here in the mountains?"

"They would say that it was a misfortune."

"Good! Rather than lose such a man as you, the

city of Hamburg would sacrifice fifteen thousand francs. Take back your box, haste away, search, gather plants, and follow your studies. Why not put that silver watch back in your pocket? It is yours, and I respect savants too much to rob them. But your country is rich enough to pay for her glory. Happy young man! You recognize, to-day, how much the title of doctor adds to your personal value. I would not have demanded a centime of ransom, if you had been as ignorant as I am."

The King listened neither to my objections, nor to Mrs. Simons' expostulations. He closed the interview, and pointed out to us the dining hall. Mrs. Simons descended to the place, all the while protesting that although she would eat her breakfast, yet she would never pay the bill. Mary-Ann seemed more depressed; but such is the mobility of youth, that she cried out with joy when she saw the place where our meal was spread. It was a little corner of green, sheltered by gray rocks. Beautiful grass formed the carpet; some clumps of privet and laurels served as hangings and hid the rocky walls. A beautiful blue arch was above our heads; birds flew back and forth in the azure vault. In a corner of our dining-hall, a limpid stream, clear as crystal, silently swept along in its course, spreading over its banks, and falling in a silvery sheet down the side of the mountain. From this side, the view illimitably extended to the sides of the Pentelicus, the great white pile which overhangs Athens; across the sad-colored olive groves; the dusty plain; the gray sides of Hymettus, rounded like an old man's spine;

and that beautiful Saronic Gulf, so blue that one might say that a strip had fallen from the sky. Assuredly, Mrs. Simons had not a mind turned to admiration, and yet, she confessed that the price for such a beautiful sight would be very high in London or Paris.

The table was laid with heroic simplicity. Brown bread, baked in a field oven, smoked upon the sod and gave out a most appetizing odor. The clotted milk quivered in a huge wooden bowl. The large olives and green piments, were laid on roughly cut pieces of wood. A shaggy goat-skin bottle spread out its large sides next to a red copper cup, roughly chiseled. An ewe's-milk cheese reposed upon the cloth which had pressed it, and which still bore its imprint. Five or six appetizing lettuces promised us a delicious salad, but there were no condiments with which to dress them. The King had placed his traveling plate at our disposal, consisting of spoons cut out with a knife, and we had, as a surfeit of luxury, our five fingers, for forks. They had not been tolerant enough to serve us with meat, but the yellow tobacco of Almyros promised me an admirable digester.

One of the King's officers served us. It was the hideous Corfuan, the man of the gold ring, who knew English. He cut the bread with his poniard and distributed it freely, praying us not to lack for anything. Mrs. Simons, without losing one stroke of her teeth, said to him in a haughty tone: "Monsieur, does your master seriously believe that we shall pay a ransom of a hundred thousand francs?"

"He is sure of it!"

"It is because he does not know the English nation."

"He knows it well, Madame, and I also. At Corfu, I have associated with many distinguished Englishmen! judges!"

"I wish you joy of it! but tell this Stavros to arm himself with patience, because he will wait a long time for the hundred thousand francs, which he has promised himself."

"He told me to tell you that he would wait for them until the 15th of May, at noon, precisely."

"And if we have not paid it the 15th of May, at noon?"

"He will regret that he will be obliged to cut off your head, as well as Mademoiselle's."

Mary-Ann dropped the bread which she was carrying to her mouth. "Give me a little wine," she said. The bandit handed to her a cup full; but scarcely had it touched her lips, before she cried out with fear. The poor child imagined that the wine was poisoned. I reassured her by emptying the cup at one draught. "Fear nothing," I said to her; "it is the resin."

"What resin?"

"Wine would not keep in these goat-skins if a certain amount of resin was not added, to prevent it from spoiling. The mixture is not very agreeable, but you may drink it without fear."

Despite my example, Mary-Ann and her mother made the bandit bring water. The man ran to the brook and was back in an instant. "You understand, Mesdames," he smilingly said, "that the King would not be foolish enough to poison such valuable people as you are." He added, turning to me: "You, M. le docteur, I have orders to tell you that you have thirty days to pursue your studies and pay the sum. I will furnish you all with writing materials."

"Thanks," Mrs. Simons said. "We will think of it in eight days, if we are not delivered before."

"And by whom, Madame?"

"By England."

"Is it far?"

"Or by the police."

"For your sake, I hope you may have that luck. In the meantime, I will do anything in my power for you."

"I wish first for a bed-chamber."

"We have near here a grotto, which is called Les Etables. You would not like it; the sheep were kept there during the winter, and the odor still remains. I will get two tents from the shepherds below and you can camp here—until the arrival—of the gendarmes!"

"I wish for a waiting-maid."

"Nothing is easier. Our men will go down to the plain, and stop the first peasant-woman who passes,—if, however, the gendarmerie will permit!"

"I must have clothes, dresses, linen, toilet appurtenances, soap, a mirror, combs, scents, a tapestry frame, a——."

"A good many things, Madame, and in order to get them all, we would be forced to go to Athens. But one will do the best. Count on me and count not too much on your soldiers."

"May God pity us!" Mary-Ann said.

A vigorous echo replied: "Kyrie Eleison!" (Lord, have mercy upon us.) It was the good old man who came to visit us, and who sang while traveling about in order to keep in practice. He saluted us cordially, placed upon the grass a vessel full of honey, and seated himself near us. "Take and eat," he said. "My bees offer you a dessert."

I shook hands with him; Mrs. Simons and Mary-Ann turned away in disgust. They obstinately refused to see him in any other light than as an accomplice of the brigands. The poor, good man knew no malice. He knew only how to chant his prayers, to care for his bees, to sell his goods, to collect the revenues of the convent, and to live at peace with the whole world. His intelligence was limited; his science, nothing; his conduct as innocent as that of a well-regulated machine. I do not believe that he was able to clearly distinguish good from bad, and to see any difference between a thief and an honest man. His wisdom consisted in making four meals a day, and of never getting more than half-seas over. He was, moreover, one of the best monks of his order.

I did full justice to the present he had brought us. This half-wild honey resembled the kind which we eat in France, as the flesh of a roe resembles lamb's meat. One would have said that the bees had distilled in an invisible alembic all the perfumes of the mountains. I forgot, in eating my bread spread with the honey, that I had only a month in which to find fifteen thousand francs, or die.

The monk, in his turn, asked permission to refresh himself a little, and without waiting for a reply, took the cup and turned out a bumper. He drank, successively, to each of us. Five or six brigands, drawn by curiosity, glided into the nook. He spoke to each by name, and drank to each, in a spirit of justice. It was not long before I cursed his presence. An hour after his arrival, half the band was seated in a circle around our viands. In the absence of the King, who was taking a siesta in his office, the brigands came, one by one, to cultivate our acquaintance. One offered his services, another brought us something, still a third introduced himself without pretext and without embarrassment, as a man who felt himself at home. The more familiar besought me to relate our history; the more timid held back at first but insensibly drew nearer. Some, having satisfied themselves with looking at us, threw themselves down, without courtesy for the ladies' presence, and immediately began to snore. And the fleas, always flying about, and the presence of their original master rendering them so bold that I surprised two or three of them on the back of my hand. Impossible to dispute their right to a grazing ground, I was no more a man, but a common pasture. At this moment, I would have given three of the most beautiful plants in my herbarium for a quarter of an hour of solitude.

Mrs. Simons and her daughter were too discreet to impart to me their views, but they proved, by some involuntary starts, that we were of a community of ideas. I even surprised a look between them which seemed to say: "The gendarmes will deliver us from the thieves, but who can deliver us from these fleas." This mute complaint awoke in my heart a chivalrous sentiment. I resolutely rose and said:

"Go away, all of you; the King has sent us here to live quietly until the arrival of our ransoms. The rent is so high that we have a right to remain alone. Are you not ashamed to crowd around a table, like parasitical dogs? You have no business here. We have no use for you; we do not want you here. Do you believe that we can escape? How? By the cascade? Or past the King's cabinet? Leave us then in peace. Coriuan, drive them away, and I will help you, if you wish."

I added action to the word. I shoved along the loiterers, I awakened the sleepers, I shook the monk. I forced the Coriuan to aid me, and soon the troop of brigands, a troop armed with poniards and pistols, gave up to us the place, with lamb-like meekness, although kicking, taking short steps, resisting with the shoulders and twisting the head, in the fashion of school-boys who have to be pushed into the school-room, when recreation is over.

At last we were alone with the Coriuan. I said to Mistress Simons: "Madame, this is our house. Will you be kind enough to separate the apartment into two divisions? I must have a little corner for my tent. Behind those trees, I shall not be badly off, and all the rest is yours, if that pleases you. You will have the brook at hand."

My offers were accepted with sufficiently bad grace. These ladies would have liked to keep all and let me go to sleep with the thieves. It is true that British conventions might have gained something by this separation, but I would have lost sight of Mary-Ann. And, moreover, I had decided to sleep far from the fleas. The Corfuan approved of my proposition, which rendered his watch less difficult. He had orders to guard us night and day. It was necessary that he should sleep near my tent, but I exacted the condition of a distance of six English feet between us.

The treaty concluded, I established myself in a corner to give chase to my domestic game. But I had scarcely begun, before the curious bandits appeared under pretext of bringing our tents.

Mrs. Simons fairly screamed when she saw that her house was composed of a simple strip of heavy felt, pleated in the middle, fastened to the earth at the two ends, and opened to the wind on two sides. The Corfuan swore that we should be lodged like princes, save in case of rain or a strong wind. The entire band began to drive in stakes, to fix our beds and to bring bed-covers. Each bed was composed of a rug with a covering made of goat-skin. At six o'clock, the King came to assure himself, with his own eyes, that we lacked nothing. Mrs. Simons, more incensed than ever, replied that she lacked everything. I formally asked for the exclusion of all useless visitors. The King established severe regulations, such as we had never followed. Discipline is a French word hard to translate in Greek. The King and his subjects retired at seven o'clock, and we were to be served then with supper. Four torches of resinous wood lighted the

THE KING OF THE MOUNTAINS. 95

table. Their red and smoky light strangely colored Miss Simons' pale face. Her eyes seemed to flash, become dim, and rekindle again, like a revolving beacon-light. Her voice, weakened by fatigue, took on, at intervals, a discordant tone. In listening to her, my mind seemed to wander in a supernatural world, and I remembered some very fantastic tales which I had once read. A nightingale sang, and I believed I saw its silvery song pouring from Mary-Ann's lips. The day had been a hard one for all, and even I, who had given substantial proof of my appetite, soon recognized the fact that I was famished only for sleep. I said good-night to the ladies and retired to my tent. In an instant, I forgot nightingale, danger, ransom, stings; I closed my eyes and I slept.

A fearful discharge of musketry awoke me with a start. I jumped up so quickly that I struck my head against the poles of my tent. At the same moment, I heard two feminine voices crying: "We are saved! The gendarmes!" I saw two or three indistinct forms rush by in the night. In my joy, in my trouble, I embraced the first shadow which passed my tent—it was the Corfuan.

"Halt!" he cried, "where are you running, if you please?"

"Dog of a thief!" I replied, "I am going to see if the gendarmes will soon finish shooting your comrades."

Mrs. Simons and her daughter, guided by my voice, came up to us. The man said to us:

"The gendarmes will not travel to-day. It is the

Ascension and the 1st of May, a double fête-day. The noise which you have heard is the signal for rejoicing. It is after midnight, almost morning; our companions go to drink wine, eat meat, dance the Romaique and burn powder. If you wish to see this beautiful sight, it will give me pleasure to take you to it. I can guard you more agreeably around the roast than at the fountain here."

"You lie!" cried Mrs. Simons, "it is the gendarmes!"

"Let us go and see," added Mary-Ann.

I followed them. The tumult was so great that one could not have slept if one had wished. Our guide led us through the King's cabinet, and we climbed to the bandit camp which was all ablaze with light. Whole pine trees, placed at intervals, were used as torches. Five or six groups, seated around a huge fire, watched the lambs roasting on spits. In the midst of the crowd, a line of dancers wound slowly around in serpentine fashion, to the measures of most frightful music. Occasional volleys of musketry were heard. Once, it came quite near us and I felt the whizzing of a ball, close to my ear. I begged the ladies to hasten forward, hoping that, near the King, we would be farther from danger. The King, seated on his ever-lasting carpet, presided with due solemnity over the diversions of his people. Around him were goat-skin bottles; the sheep were cut up and each man took a leg or shoulder and carried it about in his hands. The orchestra was composed of a rude tambourine, and a shrill flageolet. The dancers had taken off their shoes, in order to be more agile. They flounced and jumped all over the spot and came near cracking their bones, sometimes. From time to time, they left the dance, drank a cup of wine, ate a piece of meat, discharged a gun, and then returned to the dance. All these men, except the King, drank, ate, hurled themselves about and jumped; I saw not one of them even smile.

Hadgi-Stavros courteously excused himself for having awakened us.

"It is not I who am to blame, it is the custom. If the first of May passed without a discharge of musketry, these worthy people would not believe that Spring had come. I have here only simple people, brought up in the country and attached to ancient customs. I have done the best for their education that I could do, but I shall die before they become civilized. Men cannot be made over in a day like silver forks and spoons. Even I, such as you see me, have found pleasure in these gross sports; I have eaten and drunk and danced like the others. I have never known European civilization; why should I take the trouble to travel so late in life? I would give much to be young and only fifty, again. I have ideas of reform which will never be executed; I see myself, like Alexander, without an heir worthy of me. I dream of a new organization of brigandage, without disorder, without turbulence, and without noise. But I have no one to second me. I ought to have the exact census of all the inhabitants of the kingdom, with an approximate statement of their wealth, personal and real. As for the strangers who land on our shores, an agent established at each port would learn and send to me their names, their itinerary, and, as nearly as possible, their fortune. In this way, I would know what each one could give me; and I would not make the mistake of asking too little or too much. I would establish on each road a post, with proper clerks, well brought-up and well educated; because, for what good, to frighten clients with disgusting behavior or a surly mien? I have seen, in France and in England, thieves, elegant to excess; and did they not certainly succeed better because of it?

"I would demand of all my subordinates, exquisite manners, above all, from those whose business it was to accost people. I would have for prisoners of distinction like you, comfortable quarters in the open air, with fine gardens. And do not think that they would cost the occupants more dearly; to the contrary! If all those who traveled in this country were, necessarily, to fall into my hands, I could tax the passers-by for a very insignificant sum. So that each nation and each traveler would give me only a fourth per cent on their principals, I would gain upon the quantity. Then brigandage would only be a tax on the circulation; a just tax, because it would be proportional; a normal tax, because it had always been collected since ancient times. We could simplify it, if necessary, by yearly subscriptions. In consideration of a sum, once paid, one could obtain safe conduct for the natives, and an indorsed pass-port for travelers. You say that according to the terms of the Constitution no tax could be imposed without the vote of the Chambers. Ah! Monsieur, if I only had time! I would buy the whole Senate; I would nominate a Chamber of Deputies, friendly to me! A law would be passed, in a trice! One could create, if necessary, a Ministry of the Highway. That might cost me two or three millions, at first; but in four years I could square myself—, and I could keep the roads in order, into the bargain!"

He sighed heavily, then he said: "You see with what freedom I have spoken to you. It is an old habit, of which I can never break myself. I have lived, always, in the open air and in the sunlight. Our profession would be shameful if exercised clandestinely. I hide nothing about myself, but I fear no one. When you read in the papers, that search is being made for me, say without hesitation that it is a parliamentary fiction; it is always known where I am. I fear neither Ministers, the Army, nor the Tribunals. The Ministers know that by a gesture I can change a Cabinet. The Army is on my side; it furnishes me with recruits, when I need them. I receive from it, soldiers; I return, officers. As for Messieurs, the Judges, they know my opinion of them. I do not esteem them, but I pity them. Poor, and badly recompensed, one cannot expect them to be honest. I have fed some, and clothed others; I have hung very few in my life; I am, then, the benefactor of the magistracy."

He pointed out to me with a magnificent gesture, the sky, the sea, the country: "All that," said he, "is mine! Every breathing thing in the kingdom submits to me through fear, friendship or admiration. I have made many weep, and there is not one mother who would wish to have a son like Hadgi-Stavros. A day will come, when doctors, like you, will write my history, and when the isles of the Archipelago will dispute the honor of my birthplace. My portrait will hang on the walls of the houses, to keep company with the sacred images in the niches. At that time, my daughter's grandchildren will be reigning princes, who will speak with pride of their ancestor, the King of the Mountains!"

Perhaps you will laugh at my German simplicity; but this strange discourse moved me profoundly. I admired, in spite of myself, this grandeur in crime. I had not, until then, ever met a majestic rascal. This devil of a man, who might cut off my head at the end of a month, almost inspired me with respect. His grand face, as if carved from marble, serene in the midst of the orgies, seemed to me like an inflexible mask of destiny. I could not restrain myself from saying: "Yes, you are, truly, a King!"

He smilingly answered:

"In truth, then, I have flatterers even among my enemies. Do not defend yourself; I can read faces, and you have looked at me since morning, as if you would like to hang me."

"Since you have asked me to be frank, I confess that I have been angry. You have asked me a most unreasonable ransom. That you can take a hundred thousand francs from these ladies, who have them, is a very natural thing, and what might be expected of you; but that you should exact fifteen thousand from me, who has nothing, it is outrageous."

"Nothing, however, is more simple. All strangers who come here are rich, because traveling costs. You pretend that you are not traveling at your own expenses; I would like to believe you. But those who have sent you here give you at least three or four thousand francs yearly. If they go to this expense, they have their reasons, because one does nothing for nothing. You represent, in their eyes, a capital of sixty to eighty thousand francs. Then, in ransoming you for fifteen thousand, they gain by it."

"But the establishment which pays me has no capital; it has only revenues. The appropriation for the Jardin des Plantes is voted every year by the Senate; its resources are limited; one has never known a parallel case; I know not how to explain it to you—you could not comprehend—"

"And when I did comprehend it," he replied in a haughty tone, "do you believe that I would take back what I have said? My words are laws; if I wish to have them respected, I must not violate them myself.

"I have a right to be unjust; I have not the right to be weak. My injustices injure others; a weakness would ruin me. If I was known to be exorable, my prisoners would endeavor to find prayers to win me, instead of endeavoring to find money to pay me. I am not one of your European brigands who are a medley of sternness and generosity, of speculation and imprudence, of cruelty without cause, and comparison without excuse, in order to end, foolishly, on the scaffold. I have said, before witnesses, that I must have fifteen thousand francs for your head. Arrange it to suit yourself; but, in some way or other, I must be paid. Listen: in 1854, I condemned two little girls who were the age of my dear Photini. They held out their arms to me, weeping, and their cries made my fatherly heart bleed. Vasile, who killed them, tried many times; his hand trembled. And yet I was inflexible, because the ransom was not paid. Do you think, after that, that I would show you grace? What purpose would it have served me to kill them, the poor things! if one learned that I sent you away for nothing?"

I dropped my head without a word in reply. I had a thousand reasons; but I knew not how to oppose them to the pitiless logic of this old executioner. He aroused me from my reflections with a friendly tap on the shoulder. "Have courage," he said to me. "I have seen death nearer to me than you are, and I carried myself like an oak. During the war of Independence, Ibrahim ordered me to be shot by seven Egyptians. Six balls failed of their duty; the seventh struck me on the forehead and glanced off. When the Turks came to pick up my body, I had disappeared in the smoke. You have, perhaps, a longer time to live than you think you have. Write to your friends in Hamburg. You have received an education; a doctor ought to have friends worth more than fifteen thousand francs. I really wish so. I do not hate you! you have never harmed me! your death would cause me no pleasure, and it would please me to believe that you will find the means for paying the money. While waiting, go and remain with the ladies. My people may drink a drop too much, and they look upon the English with eyes that say nothing good. These poor devils are condemned to an austere life, and they are not seventy years old, as I am. In ordinary times, I can keep them obedient by fatigue; but to-day, it is different; in an hour, I cannot answer for them."

In truth, a menacing circle had already formed itself around Mary-Ann, who looked at these strange figures with innocent curiosity. The brigands, crouched before her, talked in loud tones, and praised her beauty in terms that it was well she did not comprehend. The Corfuan, who was making up for lost time, held out to her a cup of wine, which she proudly repulsed.

Five or six drinkers, more inflamed than the rest, began to fight among themselves, as if to warm themselves up and toughen themselves for later and harder exploits. I made a sign to Mrs. Simons; the ladies both rose. But the moment I offered my arm to Mary-Ann, Vasile, red with wine, advanced with a staggering gait, and made as if to take hold of her. At this sight, I was furious. I jumped at the miserable cur and I made of my ten fingers a cravat for him. He clapped his hands to his belt, and gropingly felt for the handle of the knife; but before he could find it, I saw him torn from my hands and thrown ten feet away, by the powerful hand of the old King. A murmur arose from the crowd. Hadgi-Stavros raised his head and in a tone which dominated the noise, cried: "Silence! Show that you are Greeks and not Albanians!" He added in a low tone: "Make haste! the Corfuan shall not leave me; M. German, tell the ladies that I will sleep at the door of their tent."

He went with us, preceded by his pipe-bearer, who

never left him, day or night. Two or three men, inflamed with wine, made as if to follow us; he repulsed them rudely. We were not a hundred feet from the crowd, when a ball whizzed by us. The old Palikar did not deign to turn his head. He looked at me and smiled, and said in a low tone: "One must be indulgent; it is the day of the Ascension." Reaching the path, I profited by the stupidity of the Corfuan, who was tumbling along, to ask Mrs. Simons for a private interview. "I have," I said to her, "an important secret to confide to you! Permit me to come to your tent, when our spy sleeps the sleep of Noah."

I knew not whether this Biblical comparison seemed irreverent; but she dryly replied that she knew enough not to have any secrets with me. I insisted; she was firm. I told her I had found a means of freeing ourselves without impoverishing us. She threw me a glance of defiance, consulted her daughter, and at last, acquiesced. Hadgi-Stavros made easy our interview, by keeping the Corfuan near him. He had his carpet spread at the top of the natural staircase which led to our camp, placed his arms near at hand, made the pipe-bearer lie down upon his right and the Corfuan on his left.

I kept prudently within my tent until three distinct snores assured me that our guardians were asleep. The tumult had almost subsided. Two or three shots occasionally disturbed the silence of the night. Our neighbor, the nightingale, poured forth his song. I carefully crept along in the shadow of the trees, until I reached Mrs. Simons' tent. Mother and daughter were waiting for me, outside, on the damp grass. English custom forbade my entrance to the sleeping-room.

"Speak, Monsieur," said Mrs. Simons, "but be quick about it. You know that we need rest."

I replied with assurance: "Mesdames, what I have to say to you is well worth an hour of sleep. Would you like to be free in three days?"

"But, Monsieur, we shall be to-morrow, or England will not be England. Dimitri ought to have apprised my brother by 5 o'clock; my brother would see our Minister at dinner-time; orders ought to have been given at once; the soldiers are already on the way, and we shall be free in the morning, in time for breakfast."

"Let us not deceive ourselves! time passes. I do not count upon the gendarmes! Our captors speak too lightly of them, to fear them. I have always heard, that in this country, hunter and game, gendarme and brigand, are in collusion with each other. I suppose, strictly speaking, that some men may be sent to our aid; Hadgi-Stavros will see them coming and will drag us, by lonely paths, to another and more remote retreat. He knows the country, thoroughly; all the rocks are his accomplices, every bush his ally, the ravines his "fence" (receiver of stolen goods). Parnassus is leagued with him against us; he is the King of the Mountains!"

"Bravo, Monsieur! Hadgi-Stavros is God, and you are his Prophet! He would be touched to hear with what admiration you speak of him! I have already divined that you are one of his friends, seeing how he put his hand on your shoulder, as if he was speaking to you in confidence. Is it not he who has suggested the plan of escape which you have come to propose?"

"Yes, Madame, it is he; or rather, his correspondence. I found, this morning, while he was dictating to his secretaries, the infallible means of freeing us gratis. Will you write to Monsieur, your brother, to send a sum of 115,000 francs, 100,000 for you and 15,000 for me, by some safe person, say, Dimitri?"

"By your friend, Dimitri, to your friend, the King of the Mountains? Many thanks, my dear Monsieur. It is for this price that we are to be freed for nothing?"

"Yes, Madame. Dimitri is not my friend and Hadgi-Stavros would not scruple to cut off my head. But I will continue; in exchange for the money, you shall insist that the King sign a receipt."

"And a fine receipt it would be."

"With this paper, you would get back your 115,000 francs, without losing a centime, and you will see how."

"Good evening, Monsieur. Do not waste time to say any more. Since we landed in this miserable country we have been robbed by everybody. The Customs-officers robbed us; the man who drove us to Athens robbed us; our inn-keeper has robbed us; our servant, hired by the day, who is not your friend, has thrown us into the hands of these thieves; we met a respectable monk, who shared the spoils with the brigands; all the men who were drinking up there are knaves; those who sleep before our tent, to protect us, are of the same class; you are the only honest man whom we have met in Greece, and your counsels are the best in the world! but good-evening, Monsieur! good-evening!"

"In the name of heaven, Madame!—I will not attempt to justify myself, think what you will of me. Only permit me to tell you how you can get back your money."

"And how do you think I can get it back, if all the soldiers of the kingdom cannot free us? Hadgi-Stavros is, then, no longer King of the Mountains? He knows no more hidden paths? The ravines, the bushes, the rocks, are no longer his accomplices? Good-evening, Monsieur; I can testify to your zeal; I will tell the brigands that you have executed their commission; but once for all, Monsieur, good-evening!"

The good woman gave me a push by the shoulders, crying "good-evening" in so shrill a tone, that I trembled lest she should awaken our guardians, and I sorrowfully went to my tent. What a day! I went over, one by one, all the incidents which had occurred since the hour I left in pursuit of the boryana variabilis. The meeting with the Englishwomen, Mary-Ann's beautiful eyes, the attack or the brigands, the dogs, the fleas, Hadgi-Stavros, fifteen thousand francs to pay, my life at that price, the orgies of the Ascension, the balls whizzing about my ears, the drunken face of Vasile, and to crown all, Mrs. Simons' injustice. And then to be taken for a thief! Sleep, which consoled the others, did not come to my aid. All the events which had happened had over-excited me and I could not sleep. Day broke upon my miserable meditations. I followed the course of the sun as it rose in the heavens. Some confused noises followed, little by little, the silence of the night. I had not courage to look at my watch, or to turn my head to see what was passing around me. I was overcome with fatigue and discouragement. I believe if anyone had attempted to roll me down the hill, that I would not have put out my hands to stop myself. In this prostration of my faculties, I had a vision, which partook, at the same time, of a dream and an hallucination, because I was neither awake nor asleep, and my eyes were neither closed nor open. It seemed that I had been buried alive, that my felt tent was a catafalque, adorned with flowers, and that some one chanted prayers for the dead. Fears seized me; I tried to cry out; the words stuck in my throat, or the sound of them was drowned in the chants. I heard, distinctly, verses and responses, and I recognized that funeral services were being celebrated over me, in Greek. I made a violent effort to move my right arm; it was like lead. I extended my left; it yielded easily, striking against the tent and causing something like a bouquet to fall. I rubbed my eyes, I rose on my elbow, I examined the flowers, fallen from above, and I recognized in the superb specimen, the boryana variabilis. It was certainly the flower! I touched the lobated leaves, its gamosepalous calyx, its corolla composed of five oblique petals, united at the base by a staminal filament, its ten stamens, its ovary with its five loculaments; I held in my hand the queen of malvaceae! But by what chance had I found it at the bottom of my tomb? and how send it so far to the Jardin des Plantes at Hamburg? At this moment, a lively pain drew my attention to my right arm. One would have said that it was the prey of a swarm of invisible little animals. I rubbed it with my left hand, and little by little, it became normal. I had lain with it under my head for many hours, and it had become numb. I lived then, since pain is one of the privileges of life. But, then, what did that funeral chant, which rang obstinately in my ears, mean? I raised myself. Our apartment was in the same state as on the evening before. Mrs. Simons and her daughter were sleeping profoundly. A huge bunch of flowers like mine hung from the upper part of their tent. It occurred to me that I had heard that the Greeks had a custom of decorating their dwellings on the night before the first of May. These bouquets and the boryana variabilis came, then, from the munificence of the King. The funeral chant haunted me, I could still hear it. I climbed the staircase which led to the King's cabinet, and saw a more curious spectacle than any that had astonished me the evening before. An altar was set up and dressed, under the pine. The monk, clothed in magnificent pontificals, was celebrating, with imposing dignity, the divine office. Our drinkers of the night before, some standing, others kneeling in the dust, all religiously uncovered, were metamorphosed into little saints. One fervently kissed an image painted on wood, another made the sign of the cross, the most fervent bowed themselves to the ground and wiped the dust with their hair. The King's young pipe-bearer circulated through the crowd, with a plate, saying: "Give alms! He who giveth to the Church lendeth to the Lord!"

And the centimes showered upon the plate, and the ring of the coins as they fell upon the copper dish made an accompaniment to the voice of the priest and the prayers of the suppliants. When I entered the assembly of the faithful, each one saluted me with a discreet cordiality, which recalled the primitive Church. Hadgi-Stavros, near the altar, made place for me at his side. He held a large book in his hand, and judge of my surprise, when I heard him recite the lessons in a loud voice. A brigand, officiating! He had received, in his youth, two of the lower orders; he was reader. One degree more, he would have been exorcist, and invested with the power of chasing out devils! Assuredly, I am not one of those travelers who are astonished at everything, and I practice, energetically enough, the nil admirari; but I was wonder-struck and amazed before this strange spectacle. Looking on at the genuflections, listening to the prayers, one would have supposed these actors guilty, only, of a little idolatry. Their faith seemed active and their conviction profound, but I who had seen them at work and who knew how little Christ-like they were in action, I could not help saying to myself: "Who is being fooled?"

The office lasted until some minutes after noon. An hour afterward, the altar had disappeared, the men had begun to drink again, and the good old man (the monk) led them.

The King took me one side and asked me if I had written. I promised to do so at once, and he gave me reeds, ink and paper. I wrote to John Harris, to Christodule, and to my father. I supplicated Christodule to intercede for me with his old comrade, and I told him it was impossible for me to furnish fifteen thousand francs. I recommended myself to the courage and imagination of John Harris, who was not a man to leave a friend in trouble. "If any one can save me," I wrote to him, "it is you. I do not know how you can do it, but I hope in you with all my soul; you are such a hot-headed fellow! I do not count on your finding fifteen thousand francs ransom; it would be necessary to borrow them of M. Mérinay, who lends nothing. You are, moreover, too American to consent to such a bargain. Do as you please; set fire to the Kingdom; I approve of everything in advance; but lose no time. I believe that my head is weak, and that my reason will be gone before the end of the month."

As for my unfortunate father, I kept from him the facts. To what good to bring death to his soul, by telling him to what dangers I was exposed? I wrote to him, as always, the first of the month: that I was well, and I hoped my letter would find the family well. I added that I was sojourning in the mountains, that I had discovered the boryana variabilis and a young Englishwoman more beautiful and richer than the Princess Ypsoff, of romantic memory. I had not yet been able to inspire her with love, for the lack of favorable circumstances; but I would find, perhaps, some occasion when I could render her some great service or show myself to her in my Uncle Rosenthaler's uniform. But I added with a feeling of unconquerable sadness: "Who knows but that I may die a bachelor? Then, it would fall to Frantz or Jean-Nicholas to make a fortune for the family. My health is better than ever, and my strength is not yet weakened; but Greece is a traitor which makes short work of the most vigorous men. If I am condemned to never see Germany again and to die here, some unexpected death, at the end of my travels and my work, my last regret would be for my family, and my last thought of them."

The King came up just as I was wiping away a tear, and I believe that this mark of weakness made him lose some of his esteem for me.

"Come, young man, have courage! The time is not yet come to weep over yourself. What the devil! One would say that you had been assisting at your own interment. The English lady has written a letter of eight pages, and she has not dropped a tear. Go and keep her company for a little while. She needs entertainment. Ah! if you were a man of my temper! I swear to you that at your age and in your position, I would not remain long a prisoner. My ransom would be paid in two days, and I know full well who would furnish the funds. You are not married?"

"No."

"Oh, well! You do not understand? Return to your camping place and make yourself agreeable. I have furnished you a fine opportunity to get a fortune. If you do not profit by it, you will be foolish, and if you do not put me on the list of your benefactors, you will be an ingrate."

I found Mary-Ann and her mother seated near the

cascade. While waiting for their waiting-maid, which had been promised them, they were themselves endeavoring to mend their torn habits. The bandits had furnished them with thread, or rather with twine, and some needles suitable for sewing sails. From time to time they stopped their work to look with melancholy gaze upon the houses in Athens. It was hard to see the city so near, and not to be able to go there except at a cost of a hundred thousand francs. I asked them how they had slept. The curtness of their reply, proved to me that they had been discussing our interview. At this moment, I noticed Mary-Ann's hair; she was bare-headed, and after washing it at the brook, she had left it to dry in the sun. I would never have believed that any woman could possess such a profusion of soft, glossy chestnut hair. It fell in masses over her shoulders and down her back. But it did not hang in limp strings like the locks of other women who have just washed them. It fell in perfect waves, like the surface of a little lake rippled by the wind. I had never loved anyone and I ought not to have begun by falling in love with a girl who took me for a thief. But I confess that I wished, at the price of my life, to save those beautiful tresses from the clutches of Hadgi-Stavros. I conceived, while sitting there, a plan of escape, difficult but not impossible. Our apartment (so-called) had two exits, one upon the King's cabinet, or office; the other, over the precipice. To escape by the King's cabinet was absurd! It would be necessary to traverse the camp and pass the second line of defense, guarded by the dogs. There remained the precipice. In looking over into the abyss I saw that the rock, almost perpendicular, offered enough sinuous depression, with tufts of grass, with little saplings, and available shrubs of all kinds to permit one to descend without breaking one's neck. What would render flight dangerous on this side, was the cascade. The brook, which flowed through the place, formed, on the side of the mountain, a horribly glistening sheet. It would, moreover, be difficult to keep one's courage, while descending the side of the mountain safely, with a torrent of water pouring over one's head. But were there no means of turning the course of the stream? Perhaps. In examining more closely the place where we had slept, I saw that, without any doubt, the water had once traversed that spot. Our camping place was, then, only the dry bed of a torrent. I raised a corner of the carpet which was spread under our feet, and I discovered a thick sediment, left by the water. It was possible, that some day or other, an earthquake, so frequent in those mountains, had broken down an embankment; or a vein of rock, softer than the others, had given passage to the current, and the mass of waters had been thrown from its bed. A strip ten feet long and three wide, led to the side of the mountain. In order to close this sluice, open for many years, and imprison the waters in their first reservoir, only two hours work was needed. An hour more would be enough to drain off the water, and the night wind would soon dry the rocks. Our escape, the way thus prepared, would not take more than twenty-five minutes. Once at the foot of the mountain, we would have Athens before us, and the stars would serve as guides; the paths were detestable, but we would run no risk of meeting a brigand. When the King would come in the morning to make us a visit, to inquire how we had passed the night, he would see that we had passed it, running; and, as one can acquire knowledge at any age, he would learn, to his sorrow, that one cannot count on one's self, and that a cascade was a bad guard for prisoners.

This project seemed to me so marvelous, that I, at once, imparted it to the ladies. They listened, at first, as prudent conspirators listen to an irritating agent. The younger woman, however, measured, without a tremor, the depth of the ravine. "One could do it," she said. "Not alone, but with the help of a strong arm. Are you strong, Monsieur?"

I replied, without knowing why: "I shall be, if you will have confidence in me." These words, to which I attached no particular meaning, seemed, without doubt, somewhat foolish, for she blushed and turned away her head. "Monsieur," she replied, "it may be that we have judged you wrongly; misfortune embitters one. I would willingly believe that you are a worthy young man."

She might have been able to find something more agreeable to say; but she gave me this half compliment in a voice so sweet and a look so sincere, that I was moved to the depths of my soul. So true is it, that if the air is pretty, the words of a song do not matter.

She held out to me her beautiful hand, and I had already put my own out to take it, when she suddenly withdrew it, and said: "Where will you get the material for a dike?"

"Under our feet! the turf!"

"The water will wash it away."

"Not under two hours. After us, the deluge!"

"Good!" This time she gave me her hand and I was about to carry it to my lips, but she quickly withdrew it again. "We are guarded night and day, have you thought of that?"

I had not even thought of it, but I was too well on my way to recoil before any obstacle. I replied with a resolution which astonished me: "The Corfuan? I will see to him. I will tie him to a tree."

"He will cry out."

"I will kill him."

"And the arms to do it with?"

"I will steal them." To steal! to kill! it seemed natural, since I had almost kissed her hand. Judge then, Monsieur, of what I might be capable, if ever I fell in love!

Mrs. Simons listened with a certain kindness, and I believe, approved of my plan by look and gesture. "My dear Monsieur," she said to me, "your second plan is better than your first, yes, infinitely better; I would never consent to pay a ransom, even with the certainty of receiving it again, immediately. Tell me again then, if you please, what you intend to do?"

"I will tell you the whole plan, Madame. I will procure a poniard to-day. To-night, our brigands will go to sleep early, and they will sleep soundly. I will rise at ten o'clock, I will bind our guard, I will gag him, and if necessary, I will kill him. It would not be murder, it would be an execution; he merits twenty deaths instead of one. At ten and a half, I will take up fifty square feet of turf, you can carry it to the edge of the brook, and I will construct the dam; total, one hour and a half. It will take till midnight. We will labor together to hasten the work, while the wind will dry off our path. One o'clock will come; I will take Mademoiselle on my left arm, we will glide carefully to that crevasse, we will hold ourselves up by those bushes, we will reach the wild fig-tree, we will stop to rest at that green oak, we will creep along to that prominence near those red rocks, we will get down to the ravine, and we shall be free."

"Good! and I?"

That "I" fell upon my enthusiasm like a douche of water. One is not wise in all things, and I had forgotten all about saving Mrs. Simons. Returning to help her down was not to be thought of. The ascent would be impossible without a ladder. The good woman noticed my confusion. She said to me with more pity than spite: "My poor man, you see that romantic projects always fail at some point. Permit me to hold to my first idea of waiting for the gendarmerie. I am English, and I have a confirmed habit of placing my confidence in the law. I know, moreover, the soldiers of Athens; I have seen them parade in the Palace Square. They are handsome fellows and quite soldiers, for Greeks. They have long mustaches and percussion-guns. It is they, pardon me, who will liberate us."

The Corfuan's appearance prevented my reply. He brought a maid for the ladies. She was an Albanian, quite handsome, in spite of her snub nose. Two brigands, who were returning to the mountains, had forcibly taken her, as she was walking between her mother and her betrothed, all dressed in their Sunday clothes. She screamed with such agonizing cries that it would have pierced a heart of marble, but they consoled her by telling her that they would not only release her in fifteen days, but that they would also pay her. She accepted her lot bravely and almost rejoiced at the misfortune which would increase her dowry. Happy country, where the wounds of the heart are cured with five franc pieces. This philosophical servant was not of very great use to Mrs. Simons; of all the different avenues of work open to her sex, she knew only farming. As for me, she made life unbearable by the habit she had of nibbling at a clove of garlic, as a dainty bit, and through coquetry, as the ladies of Hamburg amuse themselves devouring bonbons.

The day passed without incident. The next day seemed to all of us interminably long.

The Corfuan left us not an instant alone. Mary-Ann and her mother searched the horizon for the soldiers, but saw nothing. I, who am accustomed to active life, fretted at the inactivity. I could have had the range of mountains to add to my herbarium, under guard; but a certain feeling, I knew not what, held me near the ladies. During the night, I slept little; my plan of escape obstinately haunted me. I had noticed the place where the Corfuan laid his dagger before góing to sleep; but I would have considered it treachery to have saved myself without Mary-Ann.

Saturday morning, between five and six o'clock, an unusual noise drew me towards the King's cabinet. My toilet was quickly made; I went to bed fully dressed.

Hadgi-Stavros, standing in the midst of his band, was presiding at a noisy council. All the brigands were upon the war path, armed to the teeth. Ten or a dozen coffers which I had not seen before had been piled on some wagon-frames. I divined that they contained the baggage and that our captors were preparing to leave camp. The Corfuan, Vasile, and Sophocles were contesting something at the top of their voices, and all talking together. One could hear from a distance the barking of the outside guards. A courier, in tatters, ran toward the King, crying: "The gendarmes!"

V.

THE GENDARMES.

The King appeared to be little troubled. His eyebrows were, however, drawn a little nearer together than was usual, and the wrinkles on his forehead formed an acute angle between his eyes. He asked the courier:

"Where are they?"

"Near Castia."

"How many companies?"

"One."

"Whose?"

"I do not know."

"Wait!"

A second messenger was seen running toward the King. Hadgi-Stavros cried out to him: "Is it Pericles' company?"

"I do not know; I did not see their number." A shot was heard at a distance. "Listen!" commanded the King, taking out his watch. The men were silent. Four shots followed, a minute apart. The last one was followed by a thundering detonation which resembled platoon-firing. The King, with a smile, put his watch back in his pocket.

"It is all right! Return the baggage to the storeroom, and serve me with wine of Aegina; it is Pericles' company."

He saw me just as he finished the sentence. He called to me, in a jeering tone:

"Come, Monsieur German, you are not *de trop*. It is well to rise early; one sees curious things. Your thirst has awakened you! Will you drink a glass of wine of Aegina with our brave gendarmes?"

Five minutes later three enormous goat-skin bottles were brought from some secret hiding place. A sentinel approached the King.

"Good news! They are Pericles' men!"

A few of the bandits were in advance of the troops. The Corfuan, a fine talker, skipped along by the Captain's side, his tongue running. A drum was heard; then a blue flag was seen, and sixty men, fully armed, marched in double file to the King's Cabinet. I recognized M. Pericles, because I had admired him on the promenade at Athens. He was a young officer of thirty-five, dark, a coxcomb, admired by the ladies, the best waltzer at Court, and wearing his epaulets with grace. He put up his sword, ran to the King of the Mountains, who kissed him on the mouth, saying, "Good morning, godfather!"

"Good morning, little one," the King replied, caressing his cheek with his hand. "Thou art well?"

"Yes. And thou?"

"As thou seest. And thy family?"

"My uncle, the Bishop, has a fever."

"Bring him here, I will cure him. The Prefect of Police is better?"

"A little; he sends his kind regards; the Minister also."

"What is new?"

"A ball at the Palace on the 15th. It is decided; the 'Siècle' publishes it!"

"Thou dancest, then, all the time? And what about the Bourse?"

"There is a general fall in stocks."

"Good! hast thou letters for me?"

"Yes; here they are. Photini's was not ready. She will send it by the post."

"A glass of wine: . . . . Thy health, little one!"

"God bless thee, godfather! Who is this Frank who is listening to us?"

"Nothing! A German of no consequence. Thou hast not news for us?"

"The paymaster-general sends 20,000 francs to Argos. They will pass by the Sciromian Rocks to-morrow night."

"I will be there. Will a large band be necessary?"

"Yes! the coffer is guarded by two companies."

"Good or bad?"

"Detestable! Men who are dead shots."

"I will take all my band. In my absence thou wilt guard our prisoners?"

"With pleasure. Apropos, I have the most rigid orders. Thy English prisoners have written to their Ambassador. They have called the entire army to their aid."

"And it is I who furnished them the paper!"

"It is necessary, in consequence, that I write my report. I will recount a bloody battle."

"We will write it out together."

"Yes. This time, godfather, I must be the victor."

"No!"

"Yes! I wish to be decorated."

"Thou shalt be, some other time. What an insatiable! It is only a year since I made thee Captain."

"But understand, dear godfather, that it is for thy interest to be conquered. When the world shall learn that thy band is dispersed, confidence will be restored, travelers will again pour into the country and thou wilt make thy fortune."

"Yes, but if I am conquered the Bourse will send up stocks, and I am speculating on a fall."

"That is another affair! At least, let me kill a dozen men!"

"So be it! That will harm no one. On my side I must kill ten."

"How! One will see on our return that our company is full."

"Not so! Thou shalt leave them here; I need recruits."

"In that case, I recommend to thee little Spiro, my adjutant. He is a graduate of the military school, he has been well instructed and is intelligent. The poor boy gets only 78 francs a month, and his parents are not very well satisfied. If he remains in the army he will not become a sub-lieutenant under five or six years; the staffs are complete. But let him make himself remarked in thy troop; they will offer to bribe him, and he would have his nomination in six months."

"Good for the little Spiro! Does he speak French?"

"Passably."

"I will keep him, perhaps. If he does well for me, I will include him in the enterprise; he might be a stockholder. Thou wilt receive our account rendered for the year. I give 82 per cent."

"Bravo! my eight shares will bring me more than my Captain's pay. Ah! godfather, what career is mine?"

"What dost thou risk? Thou couldst be a brigand, but for thy mother's notions. She has always pretended that thou hast lacked a vocation. To thy health! And to yours, M. German! I present to you my godson, Captain Pericles, a charming young man who knows many languages, and who will replace me during my absence. My dear Pericles, I present to thee Monsieur, who is a doctor and is valued at fifteen thousand francs. Canst thou believe that this tall doctor, all doctor as he is, has not yet found out how to pay his ransom through our English captives. The world has degenerated, little one: it was better in my day."

Thereupon, he nimbly rose and hastened to give some orders for departure. Was it the pleasure of entering on a campaign, or the joy of seeing his godson? He seemed rejuvenated; he was twenty years younger, he laughed, he jested, he shook off his royal dignity. I would never have supposed that the only event capable of cheering a brigand would be the arrival of the gendarmerie. Sophocles, Vasile, the Corfuan and the other chiefs carried the King's orders through the camp. Every one was soon ready to depart, owing to the morning's activity. The young adjutant, Spiro, and the nine men chosen from among the gendarmes exchanged their uniforms for the picturesque dress of the bandits. This was a veritable lightning-change; the Minister of War, if he had been there, would have almost been unable to have told how it was done. The newly-made brigands seemed to feel no regret for their former employment. The only ones who murmured were those who remained under the old flag. Two or three veterans loudly complained that the selection had not been well made, and that no account had been taken of seniority. A few old soldiers vaunted their exploits and laid claim to having served the required time in brigandage. The Captain soothed them as best he could, and promised them that their turn should come.

Hadgi-Stavros, before departing, gave all his keys to his representative. He showed him the grotto where the wine was kept, in the cave in which was the flour, the cheese packed in a crevice, and the trunk of a tree in which was kept the coffee. He instructed him in every precaution which was to be taken to prevent our escape and to keep possession of so splendid a sum. The handsome Pericles smilingly replied: "What dost thou fear? I am a stockholder."

At seven o'clock in the morning the King put himself at the head of his band, and the men marched forth in single file. They marched toward the north, keeping their backs to the Sciromian Rocks. They made a long detour, by a path which was easy, to the bottom of the ravine which was below our camping place. The bandits sang at the top of their voices while wading through the brook formed by the waters of the cascade as they fell into the ravine. The war-song was a story of Hadgi-Stavros' youth, consisting of four verses:

"The Clephte aux yeux noirs descend dans les plaines;
Sonfusil doré——"

"You ought to know it; the little Athenian lads sing nothing else on the way to Catechism."

Mrs. Simons, who slept near her daughter, and who was always dreaming of the gendarmes, jumped up and ran to the window, that is to say, the cascade. She was cruelly disappointed in seeing enemies, when she expected to find saviors. She recognized the King, the Corfuan, and several others. What was the most astonishing thing to her was the formidable appearance and numbers of this morning expedition. She counted sixty men following Hadgi-Stavros. "Sixty," she thought; "there only remains twenty, then, to guard us?" The idea of escape, which she had scorned the night before, now presented itself to her with some favor. In the midst of these reflections she saw the rear-guard appear, and which she had not counted. Sixteen, seventeen, eighteen, nineteen, twenty men! Then there was no one left in the camp! "We are free! Mary-Ann," she cried. The men still filed past. The band itself consisted of eighty men; ninety marched by; a dozen dogs came behind, but she took no trouble to count them.

Mary-Ann arose at her mother's call and came quickly from the tent.

"Free!" cried Mrs. Simons. "They have all left.

What did I say? all! Even a larger number has gone than was here. Let us hasten away, my daughter!"

She hurried to the top of the staircase and saw the King's camp occupied by the soldiers. The Greek flag floated triumphantly at the summit of the pine tree. Hadgi-Stavros' place was occupied by M. Pericles. Mrs. Simons threw herself into his arms in such a transport that he had hard work to free himself from her embrace.

"Angel of God!" she said to him, "the brigands have gone."

The Captain replied in English: "Yes, Madame."

"You have put them to flight?"

"It is true, Madame, that but for us they would still be here."

"Excellent young man! The battle must have been terrible!"

"Not so! a battle without tears. I had only to say a word."

"And we are free?"

"Assuredly!"

"We may return to Athens?"

"When it pleases you."

"Oh, well! let us depart at once."

"Impossible, for the moment."

"What would we do here?"

"Our duty to our conquerors; we will guard the battle ground."

"Mary-Ann, give thy hand to Monsieur."

The young English girl obeyed.

"Monsieur," said Mrs. Simons, "it is God who sends

you here. We had lost all hope. Our only protector was a young German of the middle class, a savant who gathers herbs and who wished to save us by the most preposterous means. At last, you have come! I was sure that we would be delivered by the gendarmerie. Is it not so, Mary-Ann?"

"Yes, Mamma."

"Know, Monsieur, that these bandits are the vilest of men. They began by taking everything from us."

"All?" asked the Captain.

"All, except my watch, which I took the precaution to hide."

"You did well, Madame. And they kept all that they took from you?"

"No, they returned three hundred francs, a silver traveling case and my daughter's watch."

"These things are still in your possession?"

"Certainly."

"They did not take from you your rings and your ear-rings?"

"No, Monsieur le Capitaine."

"Will you be good enough to give them to me?"

"Give you what?"

"Your rings, your ear-rings, the silver traveling case, two watches and the sum of three hundred francs."

Mrs. Simons cried out: "What! Monsieur, you would take from us the articles the bandits returned to us?"

The Captain replied with dignity: "Madame, I must do my duty."

"Your duty is to despoil us?"

"My duty is to collect all the articles for necessary conviction in the trial of Hadgi-Stavros."

"He will then be tried?"

"Since we have taken him."

"It seems to me that our jewels and our money would serve nothing, and that you have sufficient testimony to hang him. First of all, he captured two Englishwomen; what more is necessary?"

"It is necessary, Madame, that the forms of justice be observed."

"But, dear sir, among the articles which you demand there are some which I prize highly."

"The more reason, Madame, to confide them to my care."

"But if I had no watch I should never——"

"Madame, it will always give me pleasure to tell you the hour."

Mary-Ann observed in her turn that it was disagreeable to her to be obliged to give up her ear-rings.

"Mademoiselle," the gallant Captain replied, "you are beautiful enough not to need jewels. You can do better without gems than your gems can do without you."

"You are very good, Monsieur, but my silver dressing case or necessaire is an indispensable article. What one calls a necessaire is a thing with which one cannot dispense."

"You are a thousand times right, Mademoiselle. So I beg of you not to insist upon that point. Do not add to the regret with which I have already legally despoiled two so distinguished persons. Alas! Mademoiselle, we military men, we are the slaves of orders, instruments of the law, men of duty. Deign to accept my arm, I will do myself the honor of conducting you to your tent. There, we will proceed to the inventory, if you will be good enough to permit it."

I lost not one word of this conversation, and I kept silent to the end; but when I saw this rascal of an officer offer his arm to Mary-Ann in order to politely plunder her, I became enraged, and I marched up to him to tell him what I thought of him. He must have read in my eyes the exordium of my discourse, because he threw a menacing look at me, left the ladies at the staircase of their chamber, placed a sentinel there, and returned to me, saying:

"Between us two!"

He drew me, without adding a word, to the rear of the King's cabinet. There, he seated himself before me, looked me straight in the eyes, and said:

"Monsieur, you understand English?"

I confessed my knowledge. He added:

"You know Greek, also?"

"Yes, Monsieur."

"Then, you are too learned. Do you understand my godfather, who amuses himself recounting our affairs before you? That is of no importance to him; he has nothing to hide; he is King, he is responsible to no one but himself. As for me, what the devil! put yourself in my place. My position is delicate, and I have many affairs to manage. I am not rich; I have only my pay, the esteem of my chiefs, and the friendship of the brigands. A traveler's indiscretion might cost me my promotions."

"And you count on the fact that I will keep your infamies secret?"

"When I count on anything, Monsieur, my confidence is rarely misplaced. I do not know that you will leave these mountains alive, and yet your ransom may never be paid. If my godfather would cut off your head, I should be satisfied you would not talk. If, on the contrary, you should return to Athens, I counsel you, as a friend, to keep silent about what you have seen. Imitate the discretion of the late Madame la Duchesse de Plaisance, who was taken captive by Bibichi and who died ten years later without having related to any one the details of her captivity. Do you know a proverb which runs: "The tongue cuts off the head?" Meditate seriously upon it, and do not put yourself in a place to exactly verify it."

"The menace——"

"I do not menace you, Monsieur, I am a man too well brought up to resort to threats; I warn you! If you should gossip, it is not I who would avenge myself. All the men in my company adore their Captain. They are even more warmly interested in my interests than I am myself; they would be pitiless, to my great regret, to any indiscreet person who had caused me any trouble."

"What do you fear, if you have so many accomplices?"

"I fear nothing from the Greeks, and, in ordinary times, I should insist less strongly on my orders. We have, among our chiefs, some fanatics who think that we ought to treat bandits like Turks; but I have also found some who are on the right side, in case it came to an internecine struggle. The misfortune is that the diplomats would interfere, and the presence of a stranger would, without doubt, injure my cause. If any misfortune happens to me through you, do you see, Monsieur, to what you would be exposed? One cannot take four steps in the kingdom without meeting a gendarme. The road from Athens to Piraeus is under the vigilance of these quarrelsome persons, and accidents frequently occur."

"It is well, Monsieur; I will reflect upon it."

"And will keep the secret?"

"You have nothing to ask of me and I have nothing to promise. You have advised me of the danger of being indiscreet. I accept the advice and I will refrain from speaking of it."

"When you return to Germany, you may tell whatever you please. Speak, write, publish; it is of no importance. The works published against us do no harm to any one, unless, perhaps, to their authors. You are free to relate the adventure. If you paint, faithfully, what you have seen the good people of Europe will accuse you of traducing an illustrious and oppressed people. Our friends, and we have many among men of sixty, will tax you with levity, caprice, and even of ingratitude. They will recall that you have been the guest of Hadgi-Stravros and mine; they will reproach you with having broken the holy laws of hospitality. But the most pleasing thing of the whole will be, that no one will believe you. The public will place no confidence in seeming lies. Try to persuade the cockneys of Paris, of London, of Berlin, that you have seen a Captain of the standing army, embraced by a chief of banditti. A company of choice troops acting as guards to Hadgi-Stavros' prisoners, in order to give him the opportunity of capturing the army coffers! The highest State functionaries founding a stock company for the purpose of plundering travelers! As well tell them that the mice of Attica have formed an alliance with the cats, and that our sheep take their food from the wolves' mouths! Do you know what protects us against the displeasure of Europe? It is the improbability of our civilization. Happily for the kingdom, everything which will be written against us will be too unnatural to be believed. I can cite to you a little book, which is not in praise of us, although it is accurate from beginning to end. It has been read, somewhat, everywhere; in Paris they found it curious, but I know of only one city where it seemed true! Athens! I do not prevent you from adding a second volume, but wait until away; if not, there possibly might be a drop of blood on the last page."

"But," I answered, "if I should commit an indiscretion before my departure, how could you know that I was to blame?"

"You, alone, are in my secret. The Englishwomen are persuaded that I have delivered them from Hadgi-Stavros. I charge myself with keeping up the delusion until the King's return. It will be for only two days, three at the most. We are forty kilometres from the

Scironian Rocks; our friend will reach there in the night. They will make the attack to-morrow evening, and conquerors or conquered, they will be here Monday morning. We can prove to the prisoners that the brigands surprised us. While my godfather is absent, I will protect you against yourself by keeping you away from these ladies. I will borrow your tent. You ought to see, Monsieur, that I have a more delicate skin than this worthy Hadgi-Stavros, and that I ought not to expose my complexion to the changes of temperature! What would be said, on the 15th, at the Court Ball if I presented myself brown as a peasant? I must, moreover, give those poor captives the benefit of my society; it is my duty as their liberator. As for you, you will sleep here in the midst of my soldiers. Permit me to give an order, which concerns you. Ianni! Brigadier Ianni! I confide Monsieur to thy care! Place around him four guards, who will watch him night and day, accompany him everywhere, fully armed. Thou wilt relieve them every two hours. Forward!"

He saluted me with ironical politeness, and humming a tune, descended Mrs. Simons' staircase. The sentinel shouldered arms.

From that instant there began for me a purgatory of which the human mind can have little conception. Everyone knows or guesses what a prison would be; but try to imagine a living and moving prison, the four walls of which come and go, recede and approach, turn and return, rubbing hands, scratching, blowing noses, shaking, floundering about, and obstinately fixing eight great black eyes upon the prisoner. I tried to walk; my prison of eight feet regulated the step to mine. I went toward the front of the camp; the two men who preceded me stopped short, I bumped into them. This incident explained to me an inscription which I had often seen, without understanding it, in the neighborhood of camps: "Limit of Garrison!" I turned around; my four walls turned like the scenes in a theater where a change of view is required. At last, tired of this way of promenading, I sat down. My prison seated itself around me; I resembled an intoxicated man who sees his house turn. I closed my eyes; the measured step of the sentinels wearied my brain. At least, I thought if these four soldiers would but speak to me! I spoke to them in Greek; it was a seductive agent which had never failed me with sentinels. It was clear loss of time. The walls had, possibly, ears, but the use of the voice was denied them; no one spoke under arms; I attempted bribery. I drew from my pocket the money which Hadgi-Stavros had returned and which the Captain had forgotten to take from me. I distributed it to the four cardinal points of my lodge. The somber and frowning walls changed to a smiling front, and my prison was illumined as with a ray of sunlight. But five minutes later the Brigadier relieved the guards; it was just two hours that I had been a prisoner! The day seemed long! the night, eternal! The Captain had already taken possession of my tent and my bed, and the rock which served me for a resting place was not as soft as feather. A fine penetrating rain cruelly convinced me that a roof was a fine invention; and that thatches rendered a true service to society. If at times, in spite of my unpleasant surroundings, I dropped off to sleep, I was almost always awakened by the Brigadier Ianni, who ordered a change of guards. Finally, what shall I say? At night and in dreams I saw Mary-Ann and her respectable mother in the hands of their liberator. Ah! Monsieur, how I began to render justice to the good old King of the Mountains! How I retracted all the maledictions which I had hurled against him! How I regretted his kind and paternal government! How I sighed for his return! How warmly did I breathe his name in my prayers! "My God!" I cried with fervor, "give the victory to thy servant, Hadgi-Stavros! Make every soldier in the kingdom fall beneath his hand! Bring to his hands the coffer, and even to the last écus of that infernal army! And let the bandits return, that we may be delivered from the hands of the soldiers!"

As I finished this prayer, a well-sustained fire was heard in the midst of the camp. This occurred many times during the day and following night. It was only a trick of M. Pericles. In order the better to deceive Mrs. Simons and to persuade her that he was defending her against an army of bandits, he had ordered that volleys should be fired from time to time.

This pretty conceit came near costing him dear. When the brigands arrived in camp, at dawn, on Monday morning, they believed that a fight was going on with a true enemy, and they began to fire some balls, which, unfortunately, touched no one.

I had never seen a defeated army when I assisted at the return of the King of the Mountains. The sight had, for me, all the novelty of a first experience. Heaven had listened unfavorably to my prayers. The Greek soldiers had defended themselves with so much ardor that the engagement was prolonged till night. Formed in a square around the two mules which carried the treasure, they had, at first, returned a regular fire upon Hadgi-Stavros' sharpshooters. The old Palikar, despairing of killing one by one, a hundred and twenty men who would not give an inch, attacked them with bare blades. His men assured us that he had performed marvels, and the blood with which he was covered testified to it. But the bayonet had had the last word; in other words, had won the day. The troops had killed forty brigands, of which one was a dog. A regulation bullet had arrested the advancement of young Spiro, that young officer with so brilliant a future. I saw march in sixty men, overcome with fatigue, dusty, bloody, bruised, and wounded. Sophocles had been shot in the shoulder; the men were carrying him. The Corfuan and a few others had been left on the road, some with the shepherds, some in a village, and others on the bare rocks beside the path.

The band was sad and discouraged. Sophocles howled with grief. I heard some murmurs against the King's imprudence, who had exposed the lives of his men for a miserable sum, instead of peaceably plundering rich and careless travelers.

The strongest, the freshest, the most content, the gayest of the lot was the King. His face expressed the proud satisfaction of a duty accomplished. He recognized me at once in the midst of my four men, and cordially held out his hand to me. "Dear prisoner," he said, "you see a badly treated King. Those dogs of soldiers would not give up the treasure. It was their money; my trip to the Scironian Rocks brought me nothing, and I have lost forty men, without counting some wounded who cannot live. But no matter! I am well beaten. There were too many of those rascals for us, and they had bayonets. Without which———. Come! this day has rejuvenated me. I have proved to myself that I still have blood in my veins!"

And he hummed the first verse of his favorite song: "Un Clephte aux yeux, noirs———" He added: "By Jupiter (as Lord Byron said), I would not for twenty thousand francs have remained quietly at home since Saturday. That can still be put into my history. It can be said that, at more than sixty years of age, I fought with bare sabre in the midst of bayonets; that I killed three or four soldiers with my own hand, and that I marched ten leagues in the mountains in order to return in time to take my cup of coffee. Cafedgi, my child, do thy duty! I have done mine. But where the devil is Pericles?"

The charming Captain was still resting in his tent. Ianni hurried away to bring him forth, half asleep, his mustache uncurled, his head carefully tied up in a handkerchief. I know of nothing which will so thoroughly awaken a man as a glass of cold water or bad news. When M. Pericles learned that the little Spiro and two other soldiers had been left behind, it was truly another defeat. He pulled off his handkerchief, and but for the respect he had for his person he would have torn his hair.

"This will do for me," he cried. "How explain their presence among you? and in bandit dress, too! They will be recognized! The others are masters of the battle ground. Shall I say that they deserted in order to join you? That you made them prisoners? The question will be asked why I said nothing about it. I have waited for thy coming to make my final report. I wrote last evening that I had thee almost surrounded on Parnassus, and that all our men were admirable. Holy Virgin! I shall not dare to show myself Sunday at Patissia! What will be said the 15th at the Court Ball? The whole diplomatic corps will talk me over. They will convene the council. Will I yet be invited?"

"To the council?" asked the bandit.

"No; to the Court Ball!"

"Dancer! Go!"

"My God! my God! who knows what will be done? If the only trouble was about these Englishwomen, I would not worry myself. I would confess everything to the Minister of War. These English! That was enough! But to lend my soldiers to attack the army box! To send Spiro into the engagement! They will point the finger at me; I shall never dance again!"

Who was it who rubbed his hands in glee during this monologue? It was the son of my father, surrounded by his four soldiers!

Hadgi-Stavros, quietly seated, enjoyed his coffee in little sips. He said to his godson: "Thou seemest much troubled! Remain with us. I assure thee a minimum of ten thousand francs a year, and I will enroll thy men. We will take our revenge together."

The offer was alluring. Two days before it would have received much approval. And even now it caused a faint smile among the soldiers, none from the Captain. The soldiers said nothing; they looked at their old comrades; they eyed Sophocles' wound; they thought of the deaths of the night before, and they turned wistful faces toward Athens, as if they could inhale the, to them, sweet odor of the barracks.

As for M. Pericles, he replied with visible embarrassment:

"I thank thee, but I would need to reflect. My habits are those of a city; I am delicate in health; the winters are rigorous in the mountains; I have already taken cold. My absence would be noticed at all assemblies; I would be searched for everywhere; fine marriages are often proposed to me. Moreover, the trouble is not so great as we believe it. Who knows whether the three unfortunates will be recognized? Will news of the event arrive before we do? I will go at once to the Ministry; I will find out how matters stand. No one will come to contradict me, since the two companies have kept on their march to Argos. . . . Decidedly, I must be there; I must face the music. Care for the wounded. . . . Adieu!"

He made a sign to his drummer.

Hadgi-Stavros rose, came and placed himself in front of me with his godson, whom he dominated by a head, and said to me: "Monsieur, behold a Greek of to-day! I! I am a Greek of former days! And the papers pretend that we have progressed!"

At the roll of the drum the walls of my prison fell away like the ramparts of Jericho! Two minutes afterward I was before Mary-Ann's tent. Mother and daughter hastily arose. Mrs. Simons perceived me first, and cried out to me:

"Oh, well! are we to start?"

"Alas! Madame, we are not there."

"Where are we then? The Captain gave us word for this morning."

"How did you find the Captain?"

"Gallant, elegant, charming! A little too much the slave of discipline; it was his only fault."

"Coxcomb and scamp, coward and bully, liar and thief; those are his true names, and I will prove it to you."

"Come, Monsieur; what have the soldiers done to you?"

"What have they done to me, Madame? Deign to come with me only to the top of the staircase."

Mrs. Simons arrived there just in time to see the soldiers defile past, the drummer at the head, the bandits again installed in their places, the Captain and the King mouth to mouth, giving the last good-bye kiss. The surprise was a little too much. I had not been sufficiently considerate of the good woman, and I was punished for it, because she fainted dead away and nearly broke my arms as I caught her. I carried her to the brook; Mary-Ann rubbed and slapped her hands; I threw a handful of water in her face. But I believe that it was fury which revived her.

"Miserable wretch!" she cried.

"He has plundered you, is it not true? Stole your watches, your money?"

"I do not regret my jewels; he may keep them! But I would give ten thousand francs to get back the handshakes I have given him. I am English, and I do not clasp hands with every one!" This regret of Mrs. Simons drew from me a heavy sigh. She let fall upon me all the weight of her anger. "It is your fault," she said. "Could you not have warned me? It was only necessary to tell me that the brigands were saints in comparison!"

"But, Madame, I advised you that you must put no faith in the soldiers."

"You told me so; but you said it softly, slowly, coldly. Could I believe you? Could I divine that this man was only Stavros' jailer? That he remained here to give the bandits time to get back? That he frightened us with imaginary dangers? That he claimed to have been besieged in order to have us admire him? That he simulated the night attacks to make it appear that he was defending us? I see all now, but tell us if you have nothing to say?"

"My God! Madame, I told all I knew; I did what I could!"

"But, German, who are you? In your place an Englishman would have sacrificed his life for us, and I would have given him my daughter's hand!"

Wild poppies are very scarlet, but I was more than

that when I heard Mrs. Simons' speech. I was so troubled that I dared not raise my eyes, nor respond; neither did I ask the good woman what she meant by her words. Because, in a word, why should a person as harsh as she had shown herself to be, use such language before her daughter and before me? By what door had this idea of marriage entered her mind? Was Mrs. Simons truly a woman to award her daughter, as an honest recompense, to the first liberator? There were no signs of it. Was it not rather a cruel irony addressed to my most secret thoughts?

When I examined myself I ascertained, with legitimate pride, the innocent warmth of all my sentiments. I render this justice to myself, that the fire of passion had not raised a degree the temperature of my heart. At each instant of the day, in order to test myself, I occupied myself with thinking of Mary-Ann. I built castles in Spain, of which she was the mistress. I planned romances, of which she was the heroine and I the hero. I thought of the most absurd things. I imagined events as improbable as the history of the Princess Ypsoff and Lieutenant Reynauld. I even went so far as to see the pretty English girl seated at my right on the back seat of a post-chaise, with her beautiful arm around my long neck. All these flattering suppositions, which should have agitated deeply a soul less philosophical than mine, did not disturb my serenity. I did not experience the alternatives of fear and hope which are the symptoms of love. Never, no, never, have I felt those great convulsions of the heart which are recorded in romances. Then I did not love

Mary-Ann. I was a man without reproach. I could walk with uplifted head. But Mrs. Simons, who had not read my thoughts, was perfectly capable of deceiving herself as to the nature of my devotion. Who knows whether she did not suspect me of being in love with her daughter; whether she had not misinterpreted my trouble and my timidity; whether she had not let slip the word marriage, in order to force me to betray myself. My pride revolted against so unjust a suspicion, and I replied in a firm tone, without looking her in the face:

"Madame, if I was sufficiently fortunate to rescue you from here, I swear to you that it would not be in order to marry your daughter."

"And why, then?" she asked, in a tone of pique. "Is it because my daughter is not good enough for one to marry? I find you agreeable, truly! Is she not pretty enough, or of a good enough family? Have I brought her up improperly? Is she not a good match? To marry Miss Simons, my dear sir! it is a beautiful dream! and most difficult to be gratified!"

"Alas! Madame," I replied, "you have seriously misunderstood me. I confess that Mademoiselle is perfect, and, if her presence did not make me timid, I would tell you what passionate admiration she inspired in me the first day. It is precisely for that reason that I have not the impertinence to think that any chance could raise me to her level!"

I hoped that my humility would touch this dreadful mother. But her anger was not in the least appeased.

"Why?" she cried. "Why are you not worthy of my daughter? Answer me, then!"

"But, Madame, I have neither fortune nor position."

"A fine affair! no position! You would have one, Monsieur, if you married my daughter. To be my son-in-law, is not that a position? You have no fortune! Have we ever asked money of you? Have we not enough for ourselves, for you, and for many others? Moreover, the man who would rescue us from here, would he not receive a present of a hundred thousand francs? It is a small sum, I confess, but it is something. Will you say that a hundred thousand francs is a miserable sum? Then, why are you not worthy to marry my daughter?"

"Madame, I am not——"

"Come! What is it you are not? You are not English?"

"Oh! by no means!"

"Eh! well! you cannot believe that we are foolish enough to make a crime of your birth? Eh! Monsieur, I know very well that it is not permitted to all the world to be English! The entire earth cannot be English—at least, not for many years. But one may be an honest man and a learned man without having really been born in England."

"As for integrity, Madame, it is a virtue which we transmit from father to son. As for intelligence, I have just enough to be a doctor. But, unfortunately, I have no illusions in regard to my physical defects, and——"

"You wish to say that you are ugly? No, Monsieur, you are not ugly. You have an intelligent face. Mary-Ann, is not Monsieur's face intelligent?"

"Yes, mamma!" Mary-Ann replied. If she blushed as she answered her mother saw it better than I, for my eyes were fixed obstinately on the ground.

"Monsieur," added Mrs. Simons, "were you ten times uglier, you would not then be as ugly as my late husband. And, more than that, I beg you to believe that I was as pretty as my daughter the day I gave him my hand. What have you to say to that?"

"Nothing, Madame, except that you confuse me, and that it will not be my fault if you are not on the road to Athens to-morrow."

"What do you count on doing? This time try to find a means less ridiculous than that the other day!"

"I hope to satisfy you if you will listen to me to the end."

"Yes, Monsieur."

"Without interrupting me?"

"I will not interrupt you. Have I ever interrupted you?"

"Yes!"

"No!"

"Yes!"

"When?"

"Always! Madame, Hadgi-Stavros has all his funds invested in the firm of Barley & Company."

"With our firm?"

"No. 31 Cavendish Square, London. Last Wednesday he dictated, in our presence, a business letter to Mr. Barley."

"And you never told me before?"

"You would never give me the opportunity."

"But this is monstrous! Your conduct is inexplicable! We could have been at liberty six days ago! I will go straight to him; I will tell him our relations——"

"And he will demand of you two or three hundred thousand francs! Believe me, Madame, the best way is to say nothing to him. Pay your ransom; make him give you a receipt, and in fifteen days send to him a statement, with the following note: 'Item, 100,000 francs paid, personally, by Mrs. Simons, our partner, as per receipt!' In this way you will get back your money, without the aid of the soldiers. Is it clear?"

I raised my eyes and saw the pretty smile which broke over Mary-Ann's face as she saw through the plot. Mrs. Simons angrily shrugged her shoulders, and seemed moved only by ill-humor.

"Truly," she said to me, "you are a wonderful man! You proposed to us an acrobatic escape when we had such simple means at our command! And you have known it since Wednesday morning! I will never pardon you for not having told me the first day."

"But, Madame, will you not remember that I begged you to write to Monsieur, your brother, to send you a hundred and fifteen thousand francs?"

"Why a hundred and fifteen?"

"I mean to say a hundred thousand."

"No! a hundred and fifteen. That is right! Are you

sure that this Stavros will not keep us here when he has received the money?"

"I will answer for it. The bandits are the only Greeks who never break their word. Do you not understand that if it happened once that they kept prisoners after having received the ransom, no one would ever pay one again?"

"That is true! But what a queer German you are, not to have spoken sooner."

"You always cut me short."

"You ought to have spoken even then!"

"But, Madame——"

"Silence! Lead me to this detestable Stavros."

The King was breakfasting on roast turtles, seated with his unwounded officers under his tree of justice. He had made his toilet; he had washed the blood from his hands and changed his clothes. He was discussing, with his men, the most expeditious means of filling the vacancies made by death in his ranks. Vasile, who was from Javina, offered to find thirty men in Epinus, where the watchfulness of the Turkish authorities had put more than a thousand bandits in retreat. A Laconian wished that they might get for ready money the little band belonging to Spartiate Pavlos, who had improved the province of Mague, in the neighborhood of Calamato. The King, always imbued with English ideas, thought of forced recruiting, and of pressing into service the Attic shepherds. This plan seemed to him to possess superior advantages, as it would require no outlay of funds and he would obtain the herds into the bargain.

Interrupted in the midst of his deliberations, Hadgi-Stavros gave his prisoners a cool reception. He did not offer even a glass of water to Mrs. Simons, and she had not yet breakfasted; she fully realized the omission of this courtesy. I took upon myself the part of speaker, and, in the Corfuan's absence, the King was forced to accept my services as intermediary. I said to him that after the disaster of the evening before he would be glad to learn Mrs. Simons' decision; that she would pay, with the briefest delay possible, her ransom and mine; that the funds would be turned over the next day, either to a banker in Athens, or to some other place which he would designate, in exchange for his receipt.

"I am much pleased," he said, "that these ladies have renounced the idea of calling the Greek army to their aid. Tell them that, for the second time, anything necessary for writing will be furnished them; but that they must not abuse my confidence! That they must not draw the soldiers here! At the sight of the very first soldier who appears on the mountain, I will cut off their heads. I swear it by the Virgin of the Megaspilion, who was carved by Saint Luke's own hand."

"Do not doubt! I give my word for these ladies and myself. Where do you wish to have the sum left?"

"At the National Bank of Greece. It is the only one which has not yet gone into bankruptcy."

"Have you a safe man to carry the letter?"

"I have the good old man! I will send to the convent for him. What time is it? Nine o'clock in the morning. The reverend gentleman has not yet drunk enough to become tipsy."

"The monk will do. When Mrs. Simons' brother has turned over the sum and taken your receipt, the monk will bring you the news."

"What receipt? Why a receipt? I have never given any. When you are at liberty you will readily see that you have paid me what you owe me."

"I think that a man like you ought to transact business according to European methods. In a good administration——"

"I transact business in my own way, and I am too old to change my methods!"

"As you please! I ask it in the interest of Mrs. Simons. She is guardian of her minor daughter, and she must render account of her whole fortune."

"But that will arrange itself! I care for my interests as she does for hers. When she pays for her daughter is it a great misfortune? I have never regretted what I have disbursed for Photini. Here is the paper, the ink and the reeds. Be good enough to watch the composition of the letter. It concerns your head, too!"

I rose, abashed, and followed the ladies, who saw my confusion without knowing the cause. But a sudden inspiration made me suddenly retrace my steps. I said to the King: "Decidedly, you were right to refuse the receipt, and I was wrong in asking for it. You are wiser than I; youth is imprudent."

"What do you say?"

"You are right, I tell you. It is necessary to wait. Who knows if you will not experience a second defeat more terrible than the first. You are not as strong as at twenty years of age; you may fall a captive to the soldiers."

"I?"

"They will try you as a common malefactor; the magistrates will no longer fear you. In such circumstances a receipt for a hundred and fifteen thousand francs would be overwhelming proof. Give no weapons of justice to be turned against you. Perhaps Mrs. Simons or her heirs would join in a criminal suit to recover what had been taken from them. Never sign a receipt!"

He replied in thundering tones: "I will sign it! and two rather than one! I will sign all; as many as need signing. I will sign them always for anyone! Ah! the soldiers imagine that they will manage me easily, because once, chance, and their larger force gave them the advantage! I fall, living, into their hands, I, whose arm is proof against fatigue, and whose head is proof against bullets! I seat myself on a bench, before a judge, like a peasant who has stolen cabbages! Young man, you do not yet know Hadgi-Stavros! It would be easier to pluck up Parnassus and place it upon the summit of Taygète, than to tear me from my mountains, and place me on a court bench! Write for me, in Greek, Madame Simons' name! Good! Yours also!"

"It is not necessary, and——"

"Write! You know my name, and I am sure that you will not forget it. I wish to have yours, to hold as a souvenir."

I wrote my name as best I could in the harmonious

language of Plato. The King's lieutenants applauded his firmness without understanding that it would cost him a hundred and fifteen thousand francs. I hurried with a light heart and much pleased with myself to Mrs. Simons' tent. I told her that her money had had a narrow escape, and she deigned to smile on learning that I had pretended to be deceived in order to rob our robbers. A half hour afterward she submitted for my approval the following letter:

"My Dear Brother:—The gendarmes whom you sent to our rescue were treacherous, and fled ignominiously. I advise you to see that they are hung. They will need a gallows a hundred feet high for their Captain Pericles. I shall complain of him, especially, in the dispatch which I intend to send to Lord Palmerston, and I shall consecrate to him a portion of the letter which I shall write to the editor of the "Times," as soon as you have set us free. It is useless to hope anything from the local authorities. All the natives are leagued against us, and the day after our departure the Greeks will gather in some corner of the kingdom to divide what they have taken from us. Fortunately, they will have little. I have learned from a young German, whom I took at first for a spy, and who is a very honest man, that this Stavros, called Hadgi-Stavros, has funds placed with our firm. I beg you to verify the fact, and if it is true, let nothing prevent you from paying the ransom which is demanded. Turn over to the Bank of Greece 115,000 francs (4600 sterling) for a regular receipt, sealed with this Stavros' seal. The amount will be charged to his account. Our health is good, although life in the mountains may not be comfortable. It is monstrous that two English women, citizens of the greatest kingdom in the world, should be compelled to eat their roast without mustard and without pickles and to drink pure water like any fish.

"Hoping that you will not delay in arranging for our return to our accustomed habits, I am, my dear brother, very sincerely yours,   Rebecca Simons."

I carried, to the King, the good woman's letter. He took it with defiance, and examined it so sharply that I trembled lest he should understand it. I was, however, very sure that he knew no English. But this devil of a man, inspired me with superstitious terror, and I believed him capable of performing miracles. He seemed satisfied only when he reached the figures 4600 livres sterling. He saw, at once, that he was not to be troubled with the gendarmes. The letter was placed, with other papers, in a tin cylinder. They brought forward the good old man, who had drunk just enough wine to limber up his legs, and the King gave the box to him, with very explicit instructions. He departed, and my heart kept pace with him to the end of his journey. Horace did not follow with a more tender look the ship which bore Virgil away.

As soon as the King saw the affair in train to be completed, he became very genial. He ordered for us a veritable feast; he distributed double rations of wine to his men; he went himself to look after the wounded, and with his own hands extracted the ball from Sophocles' shoulder. Orders were given the bandits to treat us with the respect due our money.

The breakfast which I ate, without spectators, with the ladies was one of the happiest repasts I ever remember. All my evils were then ended; I should be free after two days of this sweet captivity. Perhaps even, on leaving Hadgi-Stavros, an adorable slavery! . . . I felt that I was a poet like Gessner. I ate as heartily as Mrs. Simons, and I assuredly drank with more appetite. I gulped down the white wine of Aegina, as formerly the wine of Santorin. I drank to Mary-Ann's health, to her mother's, to my good parents' and to that of Princess Ypsoff. Mrs. Simons wished to hear the history of that noble stranger, and by my faith, I did not keep it secret. Good examples are never too well known. Mary-Ann gave charming attention to my recital. She thought that the Princess had done well, and that a woman ought to take her happiness wherever she found it. Proverbs are the wisdom of nations, and sometimes their success. I was cast upon the wind of prosperity, and I felt myself borne toward, I know not what terrestrial paradise. Oh, Mary-Ann! the sailors who traverse the ocean have never had for guides two stars like your eyes!

I was seated before her. Passing the wing of a fowl to her, I leaned so near her that I saw my image reflected in her eyes. I found I looked well, Monsieur, for the first time in my life! The frame set off the picture so well. A strange thought seized me. I felt that I had surprised, in this incident, a decree of destiny. It seemed to me that the beautiful Mary-Ann carried in the depths of her heart the image which I had discovered in her eyes.

All this was not love, I know it well, I wish neither to accuse myself, nor to appropriate to myself a sentiment which I have never felt; but it was a firm friendship, and which would suffice, I thought, for a man about to enter the wedded state. No turbulent emotion stirred my heart, but I felt it melting slowly like a piece of wax in the warmth of a genial sun.

Under the influence of this reasonable ecstasy, I related to Mary-Ann and her mother the history of my life. I described to them the paternal mansion, the great kitchen where we all ate together; the copper sauce-pans hanging on the wall according to size; the strings of hams and sausages which hung in the inside of the chimney; our modest, and often hard life: the future of each of my brothers; Henri ought to succeed papa; Frederic was learning the tailor's trade; Frantz and Jean-Nicholas had had positions since they were eighteen; the one as corporal, the other, as quarter-master sergeant. I told them of studies, my examinations, the little successes which I had enjoyed at the University, the beautiful future of professor to which I could lay claim, with three thousand francs income, at least. I do not know to what point my recital interested them, but I took great pleasure in it, and I stopped to drink from time to time.

Mrs. Simons did not speak to me again about our discussion on marriage, and I was very happy. It is better not to say a word, than to talk in the air when we know ourselves so little. The day passed for me, like an hour; I mean as an hour of pleasure. The next day seemed long to Mrs. Simons; as for me, I would have liked to stop the sun in its course. I instructed Mary-Ann in the first principles of botany. Ah! Monsieur, the world does not know all the tender and delicate sentiments one can express in a lesson in botany.

At last, on Wednesday morning, the monk appeared on the horizon. He was a worthy man, taken altogether, this little monk! He had risen before dawn in order to bring us liberty in his pocket. He brought to the King a letter from the president of the bank, and to Mrs. Simons a letter from her brother. Hadgi-Stavros said to Mrs. Simons: "You are free, Madame, and you may take Mademoiselle, your daughter, away. I hope that you will not take away from our rocks too unpleasant memories. We have offered you all that we have; if the bed and the table have not been worthy of you, it is the fault of circumstances. I had this morning an angry fit, which I pray you to forget; one must pardon a conquered general. If I dared to offer a little present to Mademoiselle, I would beg her to accept an antique ring which could be made to fit her finger. It does not come from any plunder we have taken; I bought it of a merchant of Nauplie. Mademoiselle will show this jewel in England, in relating her visit to the King of the Mountains."

I faithfully translated this little speech, and I slipped the King's ring on Mary-Ann's finger, myself.

"And I," I asked of Hadgi-Stavros, "shall I carry away nothing by which to remember you?"

"You, dear sir? But you remain! Your ransom is not paid!"

I turned toward Mrs. Simons, who held out to me the following letter:

"Dear Sister:
Verification made, I have given the 4000. liv. sterl. for the receipt. I have not advanced the other 600, because the receipt was not in your name, and it would be impossible to recover it. I am, while waiting your dear presence,   Always yours,
                        "Edward Sharper."

I had overdone my instructions to Hadgi-Stavros; to be quite business-like, he believed that he ought to send two receipts!

Mrs. Simons said to me in a low tone: "You seem to be in great trouble! What good will it do to make such faces? Show that you are a man, and leave that grievance for a whipped cur. The best part is done, since we are saved, my daughter and I, without its costing us anything. As for you, I am not uneasy about you; you know how to save yourself. Your first plan, which was not feasible for two ladies, will be an admirable one for you alone. Come, what day may we expect a visit from you?"

I thanked her cordially. She offered such a fine opportunity for me to show off my personal qualities and to raise myself in Mary-Ann's esteem. "Yes, Madame, count on me! I will leave here a man of spirit, and much better if I run a little danger. I am glad that my ransom has not been paid, and I thank Monsieur, your brother, for what he has done for me. You will see if a German does not know how to extricate himself from difficulties. Yes, I will soon bring you my own messages!"

"Once out of here, do not fail to present yourself at our hotel."

"Oh! Madame!"

"And now beg this Stavros to give us an escort of five or six brigands."

"In God's name why?"

"To protect us from the gendarmes!"

VI.

THE ESCAPE.

In the midst of our adieux, there came to us a powerful odor of garlic which made me ill. It was the waiting-maid who had come to the ladies, to call upon their generosity. This creature had been more annoying than useful, and since the first two days, the ladies had dispensed with her services. Mrs. Simons regretted, however, not being able to do anything for her, and asked me to inform the King how she had been robbed of her money. Hadgi-Stavros seemed neither surprised nor scandalized. He simply shrugged his shoulders, and muttered: "That Pericles!—bad education—the city—the court—I ought to attend to that." He added out loud: "Beg the ladies to not trouble themselves about anything. It is I who provided the servant and it is I who will pay her. Tell them, that if they need a little money to return to the city, my purse is at their disposal. I will have them escorted to the foot of the mountain, although they will run no kind of danger. The soldiers are less to be feared than one thinks. They will find breakfast, horses and a guide in the village of Castia: everything is provided and everything paid. Do you think that they will give me the pleasure of shaking hands with me, in token of reconciliation?"

Mrs. Simons was very reluctant, but her daughter resolutely held out her hand to the old Palikar. She said to him in English, with roguish pleasantry: "It is much honor that you do us, very interesting, sir, because at this moment we are the Clephtes, and you are the victim!"

The King replied with much confidence: "Thank you, Mademoiselle; you are too good!"

Mary-Ann's pretty hand was colored like a piece of rosy satin which had been in a shop-window for three months. Believe, however, that I did not have to beg to kiss it. I then touched my lips to Mrs. Simons' skinny hand. "Courage! Monsieur," cried the old lady as she was going away. Mary-Ann said nothing; but she threw me a glance capable of rousing an army. Such looks are worth a proclamation!

When the last man of the escort had disappeared, Hadgi-Stavros took me to one side and said to me: "Eh, well! we have then made some mistake!"

"Alas! Yes, we were not clever."

"This ransom is not paid. Will it be? I believe so. These English women seem to be friendly to you."

"Be not uneasy: within three days I shall be far from Parnassus."

"All right, so much the better. I have great need of money, as you know. Our bad luck on Monday will tax our income heavily. We must make up our personal and material losses."

"You can complain with good grace. You have obtained a hundred thousand francs at one stroke!"

"No, ninety! the monk has already taken his tithe. Of that sum, which seems enormous to you, there will be only twenty thousand for me. Our expenses are considerable; there are heavy charges. What would be done if the company of stock-holders should decide to build a Hotel des Invalides, as has been talked of? There are always pensions to be paid to the widows and orphans of the band. Fever and bullets yearly relieve us of thirty men, and you can see where that places us. Our expenses would scarcely be met; I should have to pay money out of my own pocket, my dear sir!"

"Have you never happened to lose more than once?"

"Once, only. I had received fifty thousand francs on account, of the society. One of my secretaries, whom I afterward hung, fled to Thessaly with the sum. I had to make up the deficit: I was responsible. My share amounted to seven thousand francs; I lost, then, forty-three thousand. But the knave who stole from me paid dearly. I punished him according to the Persian mode. Before hanging him, his teeth were pulled, one after the other, and they were driven, with a mallet, into his cranium—for a good example, you understand. I am not wicked, but I suffer no one to put me in the wrong."

It rejoiced my heart that the old Palikar, who was not wicked, should lose the eighty thousand francs of Mrs. Simons' ransom, and that he would receive the news when my cranium and my teeth were not in his camp. He put his arm through mine, and said familiarly:

"How are you going to kill the time till your departure? These ladies are gone and the house will seem large. Do you wish to look at the Athenian papers? The monk brought some to me. I rarely read them. I know exactly the price the articles are worth, since I pay for them. Here you will find the Gazette officielle, l'Esperance, Pallicare, Caricature. Each one ought to speak of us. Poor readers! I leave you. If you find anything curious, tell me about it."

L'Esperance, printed in French, and intended to fool Europe, devoted a long article to denying the latest news of brigandage. It cleverly joked the simple travelers who saw a thief in every ragged peasant, an armed band in every cloud of dust, and who asked pardon of the first thorn-bush on which their clothes were caught. This truth-telling sheet vaunted the security of the roads, celebrated the disinterestedness of the natives, exalted the quiet and seclusion which one was sure of finding on all the mountains in the kingdom.

The Pallicare, printed under the supervision of some of Hadgi-Stavros' friends, contained an eloquent biography of its hero. It recounted that this Thesseus of modern times, the only man in our century who had never been vanquished, had made a sortie in the direction of the Scironian Rock. Betrayed by the weakness of his companions, he had withdrawn with small loss. But seized with profound distaste for a degenerate profession, he had renounced, henceforth, the practice of brigandage, and had left Greece; he had exiled himself in Europe, where his fortune, gloriously acquired, would enable him to live like a prince. "And now," added the Pallicare, "go, come, travel across the plain and in the mountain! Bankers and

Merchants, Greeks, strangers, travelers, you have nothing to fear; the King of the Mountains wished, like Charles V., to abdicate at the height of his glory and power."

The Gazette officielle read as follows:

"Sunday, 3d instant, at 5 o'clock in the evening, the military chest containing 20,000 francs, which a large company was guarding on its way to Argos, was attacked by the band of Hadgi-Stavros, known as the King of the Mountains! The brigands, to the number of three or four hundred, fell upon the soldiers with incredible ferocity. But the first two companies of the second battalion of the 4th Line, under the command of the brave Nicolaïdis, opposed them with a heroic resistance. The savage attacking party were repulsed at the point of the bayonet and left the field covered with the dead. Report has it that Hadgi-Stavros was seriously wounded. Our loss was insignificant.

"The same day, and the same hour, Her Majesty's troops were victors in another skirmish, about ten leagues distant. It was at the summit of Parnassus, four furlongs from Castia, that the 2d Company of the 1st Battalion of gendarmes defeated Hadgi-Stavros' band. There, according to the report of the brave Captain Pericles, the King of the Mountains was wounded. Unfortunately, this success was dearly bought. The brigands, protected by the rocks and shrubs, had killed or seriously wounded ten of the soldiers. A young officer, M. Spiro, graduate of the Erelpides School, died a heroic death on the field of battle. In the presence of such great misfortunes, it is no mean consolation that there, as everywhere, the law reigns."

The journal La Caricature contained a badly printed lithograph, in which I recognized, however, Captain Pericles and the King of the Mountains. The godson and godfather were holding each other in close embrace. Below this cartoon, the artist had written the following sentence:

"This Is How They Fought!"

"It seems," I said to myself, "that I am not alone in their confidence, and that Pericles' secret is an open secret."

I folded up the papers, and while waiting the King's return, I meditated upon the position in which Mrs. Simons had left me. Surely, it was fine to owe my freedom to no one but myself, and much braver to leave a prison by a feat of courage, than by a schoolboy's trick. I could, in a day or two, become a hero of romance, and the object of admiration of all the young girls in Europe. No doubt Mary-Ann would adore me when she saw me safe and sound after so perilous an escape. I might make a misstep in that slippery path. What if I broke a leg or arm! Would Mary-Ann look with favor on a lame and crippled man? I must, moreover, expect to be guarded night and day. My plan, ingenious as it was, could be executed only after the death of my guard. To kill a man is no small affair, even for a doctor. It is nothing in words, especially when one speaks to the woman whom one loves. But, since Mary-Ann's departure, I was no longer deranged. It seemed less easy to procure a weapon and to use it. A poniard thrust is a surgical operation which ought to make an honest man's flesh creep. What do you say, Monsieur? I think that my future mother-in-law had treated her hoped-for son-in-law very contemptuously. It would not have cost her much to have sent me 15,000 francs ransom, taking them, later, out of Mary-Ann's dowry. Fifteen thousand francs would have been of little value to me the day of my marriage. It seemed of much account in the condition in which I found myself, on the eve of murdering a man, and descending some hundreds of meters by a ladder without any rungs. I cursed Mrs. Simons as heartily as the generality of sons-in-law curse their mothers-in-law in all civilized lands. As I had maledictions to spare, I directed some of them against my friend John Harris, who had abandoned me to my lot. I said to myself, that if we could have exchanged places, that I would never have left him eight days without news.

I excused Lobster, who was very young; and Giacomo, who was not very intelligent, and also M. Mérinay, whose downright selfishness I fully understood. One easily pardons treason in such egotists, because one never counts on them. But Harris, who had risked his life to save an old negress in Boston! Was I not of as much account as a negress? I believed, in truth, without any aristocratic prejudices, that I was worth two or three times as much.

Hadgi-Stavros came to change the course of my thoughts by offering a means of escape more simple and less dangerous. It was only necessary to have legs, and, thank God! I was not lacking in that particular. The King surprised me just as I was yawning fearfully.

"Do you feel dull?" he asked. "It is the reading. I never can open a book without fear of dislocating my jaws. I am pleased to see that doctors cannot endure it any better than I. But why not employ the time you remain to better advantage? You came here to gather the mountain plants; your box has received nothing these eight days. Would you like to search for some, under guard of two men? I am too good a fellow for you to refuse this little favor. Each must pursue his course in this lower world. You collect plants; I, money. You can say to those who sent you here: 'Here are plants gathered in Hadgi-Stavros' Kingdom!' If you find one which is beautiful and strange, and of which one has never heard in your country, you must give it my name, and call it the Queen of the Mountains!"

"But truly," I thought, "if I was a league from here, with two brigands, would it not be possible to outstrip them? There was no doubt but that danger would give me double strength. He who runs best is he who has the most to gain! Why is the hare the swiftest of all animals? Because he is the most terrified!"

I accepted the King's offer, and, on the spot, he placed two guards over me. He gave them no minute instructions. He simply said:

"Here is milord, worth 15,000 francs; if you lose him, you will have to bring him back or pay the sum."

My attendants did not look like invalids; they had neither wounds, bruises, nor injury of any sort; their muscles were like steel, and it was not to be expected that they would be retarded by any constraint of their foot-gear, because they wore large moccasins, which left their heels bare. Passing them in review, I noticed, not without regret, two pistols as long as children's guns. I, however, did not lose courage. By reason of keeping bad company, the whizzing of bullets had become familiar to me. I slung my box over my shoulder and started.

"Much pleasure to you!" cried the King.

"Adieu! Sire!"

"Not so, if you please; au revoir!"

I drew my companions in the direction of Athens; it was so much gained from the enemy. They made no resistance, and allowed me to go where I wished. These bandits, much better brought up than Pericles' four guards, allowed me plenty of room. I did not feel, at each step, the point of their elbows in my ribs. They picked on the path green stuff for the evening meal. As for me, I appeared very eager in my work; I pulled up, on the right hand and on the left, tufts of grass of no account; I pretended to choose a sprig from the mass, and I placed it very carefully in the bottom of my box, taking care not to overload myself; it was enough of a burden that I carried. I had once known, at a horse race, of a jockey who was beaten because he carried a burden weighing five kilogrammes. My gaze seemed fixed upon the ground, but you can well believe that the interest was feigned. Under such circumstances one is not a botanist, one is a prisoner. Pellison would never have amused himself with spiders if he had had a file with which to saw his bars. I may have, perhaps, seen that day unknown plants which would have made a naturalist's fortune; but I troubled myself no more about them than as if they had been common wall-flowers. I am sure that I passed near a fine specimen of the boryana variabilis! It would have weighed a half-pound with its roots. I did not even honor it with a look. I saw only two things: Athens in the distance, and the two brigands on either side. I secretly watched the rascals' eyes, in the hope that something would distract their attention; but, whether they were right at hand or ten feet away, whether they were occupied in picking their salads or following the flight of the vultures, they kept an incessant watch on my movements.

An idea came to me to give them serious occupation. We were in a narrow path, which evidently led towards Athens. I saw at my left a beautiful bunch of broom which grew on the top of a rock. I pretended to be eager to secure it as a treasure. I made five or six attempts to scale the precipitous bowlder on which it blossomed. I seemed so determined to reach it that one of my guards offered himself as a short ladder. This was not exactly what I had counted on. I felt obliged to accept his services, but, in climbing upon his shoulders, I hurt him so cruelly with my hob-nailed shoes, that he groaned with agony and let me drop to the ground. His comrade, who was interested in the process of the enterprise, said to him: "Wait! I will mount instead of milord, I have no nails in my shoes." No sooner said than done; he sprang up, seized it by the stalk, shook it, pulled it, tore it up by the root and cried out. I was already running away, without looking behind. Their stupefaction gave me a good ten seconds' advantage. But they lost no time in accusing each other, for I soon heard them following me. I redoubled my efforts; the path was a good one, even, smooth, made for me. We descended a steep declivity. I ran desperately, my arms pressed to my sides, without noticing the stones which rolled under my heels, or looking to see where I put my feet. I fairly flew over the path; rocks and bushes on either side seemed to be running in the opposite direction; I was light-footed, I was supple, my body weighed little; I had wings. But the four foot-falls wearied my ears. Suddenly, they ceased; I heard nothing more. Had they become weary of following me? A little cloud of dust rose ten steps ahead of me. A little further on, a white spot suddenly appeared on a gray rock. I heard two detonations at the same instant. The brigands had discharged their pistols! I was not hit, and I still sped on. The pursuit began again; I heard the breathless voices calling to me: "Stop! Stop!" I did not stop. I lost the path, but I still ran on, not knowing where I was going. A ditch as wide as a river presented itself; but I was flying too fast to measure distances. I jumped, I was saved!—my suspenders broke!—I was lost!

You laugh! I would like to see you run without suspenders, holding in both hands the band of your trousers! Five minutes afterward, I was again a captive. The men hand-cuffed me, fettered my legs, and drove me with switches to Hadgi-Stavros' camp.

The King treated me as a bankrupt who had carried away 15,000 francs. "Monsieur," he said to me, "I had a better opinion of you. I thought I knew honest men! your face deceived me. I would never have believed that you were capable of doing wrong, above all, after the way in which I have treated you. Do not be astonished if I, henceforth, use severe measures; you have forced me to do so. You will remain in your chamber until further orders. One of my officers will remain with you under your tent. This is only a precaution. In case of a repetition of the offense, it is punishment which will be given you. Vasile, it is to thee I commit Monsieur."

Vasile saluted me with his usual courtesy.

"Ah! wretch!" I thought, "it is thou who throwest infants into the fire! It is thou who wouldst have embraced Mary-Ann; it is thou who wouldst have stabbed me on Ascension Day. Oh, well! I prefer to settle with thee rather than with another!"

I will not relate to you the details of the three days I passed in my tent with Vasile. The scamp gave me a dose of disgust which I do not wish to share with anyone. He did not wish me any ill; he even had a certain sympathy for me. I believe that if I had been his own prisoner, that he would have released me without ransom. My face had pleased him at first sight. I recalled to him a younger brother who had been condemned to death and hanged. But these friendly overtures wearied me a hundred times more than bad treatment. He did not wait until sunrise to say "good-morning" to me; at night-fall, he never missed a long list of successes which he wished me. He aroused me, in my deepest sleep, to ascertain if I was well covered. At table, he gave me good service; at dessert he begged of me to listen to some stories which he wished to relate. And always that hand was before me ready to shake mine. I fiercely opposed his advances. It seemed to me unnecessary to include a roaster of infants in my list of friends, and I had no desire to press the hand of a man whom I had condemned to death. My conscience permitted me to kill him; was it not a case of legitimate defense? but I did have scruples about killing him treacherously, and I ought, at least, to put him on his guard by hostile and menacing attitude. While repulsing his advances, his kindness, and repelling his polite attentions, I carefully watched for a chance to escape; but his friendship, more vigilant than hate, did not lose sight of me for an instant. When I hung over the cascade in order to impress upon my mind the unequal places in the bank, Vasile would draw me from my contemplation with maternal solicitude: "Take care!" he would say to me, pulling me back by the feet! "if thou shouldst fall by some unhappy chance, I should reproach myself all my life." When, at night, I stealthily tried to rise, he jumped from his bed, asking if I needed anything. Never was there a more watchful rascal. He turned around me like a squirrel in a cage.

What, above everything, made me despair, was the

confidence he had in me. I expressed, one day, a desire to examine his arms. He placed his dagger in my hand. It was Russian blade, of inlaid steel, from the famous sword factory of Toula. I drew it from its sheath, I tried the point with my finger, I turned it toward his breast, choosing the place between the fourth and fifth ribs. "Do not press on it, thou mightest kill me!" Truly, by pressing on it a little, I could have given him his just desserts, but something stayed my hand. It is to be regretted that honest men recoil from killing assassins, when the latter feel no compunctions about killing honest people. I put the weapon back into its case. Vasile held out his pistol to me, but I refused it, and I told him that my curiosity was satisfied. He cocked it, he made me look at the priming, he placed it on his head, and said to me: "See! thou art no longer guarded!"

No longer guarded! eh! parbleu! that was exactly what I wished. But the occasion was too good a one, and the traitor paralyzed me. If I had killed him at such a moment, I would not have felt equal to enduring his last look. Much better to give the blow in the night. Unfortunately, instead of hiding his arms, he placed them ostensibly between his bed and mine.

At last, I conceived a plan for escaping, without awakening him or killing him. The idea flashed across my mind, Sunday, the 11th day of May, at 6 o'clock. I had noticed, on Ascension Day, that Vasile loved to drink, and that it took but little wine to intoxicate him. I invited him to dine with me. This exhibition of friendship mounted to his brain; the wine of Aegina did the rest! Hadgi-Stavros, who had not honored me with a visit since I had lost his esteem, still acted as a generous host. My table was better served than his own. I could have drunk a goat-skin of wine or a cask of rhaki. Vasile, admitted to his share of these luxuries, began the repast with touching humility. He kept three feet from the table, like a peasant invited to his master's house. Little by little, the wine lessened the distance. At eight o'clock, my guardian explained his character to me. At nine, stutteringly related to me the adventures of his youth, and a series of exploits which would have made a Criminal Examining Magistrate's hair stand on end. At ten, he became philanthropic; this heart of tempered steel was dissolving in the rhaki, like Cleopatra's pearl in the vinegar. He swore to me that he became a bandit because of his love for humanity; that he would make his fortune in ten years, would found a hospital with his savings, and then retire to a monastery on Mount Athos. He promised that he would not forget me in his prayers. I took advantage of his good intentions in order to make him drink an enormous cup of rhaki. I might have offered him boiling pitch; he was too much my friend to refuse me. Soon, he lost his voice; his head swung from the right to the left, from the left to the right, with the regularity of a pendulum; he held out his hand to me; it alighted on the remains of the roast, this he shook cordially, fell over on his back, and slept the sleep of the Egyptian Sphinx, which the French cannons have never awakened.

I had not an instant to lose; the minutes were

golden. I took his pistol, which I threw to the bottom of the ravine. I seized his dagger, and was going to throw that down also, when the thought came to me that it would be useful in cutting up the turf. My watch showed eleven o'clock. I extinguished the two torches of resinous wood which had lighted our table; the light might attract the King's attention. It was a beautiful night. No moon at all, but the sky was studded with stars; it was just the kind of night for my purpose. The turf, cut in long strips, came up like cloth. I had a sufficient quantity at the end of an hour. As I carried them to the spring, I stumbled against Vasile. He raised himself, heavily, and through habit, asked me if I needed anything. I let fall my burden and seated myself near the drunken man, and begged him to drink one more cup to my health. "Yes!" he mumbled, "I am thirsty." I filled for him the copper cup for the last time. He drank half of it; spilled the remainder over his face and neck, attempted to get up, fell over on his face, with his arms extended, and moved no more. I ran to my dike, and novice as I was, the brook was solidly dammed up in forty-five minutes; it was a quarter of one o'clock. To the noise of the cascade succeeded a profound silence. Fear seized me. I reflected that the King probably slept lightly, like most old people, and that the unusual silence would probably awake him. In the tumult of thoughts which filled my mind, I remembered a scene in the Barbier de Seville, where Bartholo was awakened when he ceased to hear a piano. I glided under the trees to the staircase, and looked toward the King's cabinet. He was sleeping peacefully beside his pipe-bearer. I crept stealthily along within twenty feet of his tree, I listened; all were asleep. I went back to my dam, passing through a puddle of icy water, which was already up to my ankles, flung myself down and looked over the abyss. The side of the mountain had gradually become polished. There were, here and there, cavities in which water had formed in pools. I had taken accurate note; these places were where I could put my feet. I returned to my tent, took my box which was suspended over my bed, and slung it over my shoulders. In passing the place where we had dined, I picked up a part of a loaf, and a piece of meat which the water had not yet wet. I put these provisions in my box for my breakfast next morning. The dam still held well, the wind ought to have dried my path; it was nearly two o'clock. I wished, in case of an encounter with any one, to take Vasile's dagger, but it was under the water and I could lose no time searching for it. I took off my shoes, I tied them together, and hung them on the strap of my box. At last, after thinking of everything, throwing a last look at my earthworks, giving a thought to my family at home, and sending a kiss in the direction of Athens and Mary-Ann, I threw one leg over the edge, I seized with both hands a tree which hung over the abyss, and I started out, trusting to God to help me.

It was rough work, harder than I had supposed when looking down. The rock, not entirely dry, gave me a feeling of clammy cold, like the contact of a serpent. I had not calculated distances accurately, and the points of support were farther apart than I had hoped. Twice I took a wrong course in moving to the left. I had to return, a work of incredible difficulty. Hope abandoned me often, but not my will. My foot slipped; I mistook a shadow for a projection, and I fell fifteen or twenty feet, clinging with my hands and body to the side of the mountain, without finding a place to stop myself. A root of a fig-tree caught me by the cuff of my coat-sleeve, you can see the marks here. A little further on, a bird, hidden in a little hole, on the mountain side, flew out between my legs so suddenly, and frightened me so, that I almost fell head first. I advanced with feet and hands, especially with my hands. My arms seemed broken, and I heard the tendons creak like the cords of a harp. My nails were so cruelly torn that they ceased to pain me. Perhaps, if I had been able to measure the distance still before me, I would have felt renewed strength; but when I turned my head, I became so dizzy that I abandoned the attempt. To sustain my courage, I talked to myself; I spoke out loud between my clenched teeth. I said: "One more step for my father! yet another for Mary-Ann! still one more for the confusion of the brigands and the rage of Hadgi-Stavros!"

My feet at last rested on a broad ledge. It seemed to me that the soil had changed color. I bent my knees, I seated myself, I turned my head. I was only ten feet from the brook. I had reached the red rocks. The smooth stone, full of hollows, in which the water still stood, allowed me to take breath and rest a little. I drew out my watch; it was only half past two. I would have believed that my journey had taken three nights. I examined my arms and legs, to ascertain if I still possessed them all; in this kind of an expedition one never knows what will happen. I had had good luck; I had suffered some contusions and the skin was rubbed off in two or three places. The worst sufferer was my paletot. I looked up, not to thank Heaven, but to assure myself that nothing had moved in my camping place. I heard only the drops of water filtering through my dam. All was well; I was reassured; I knew where to find Athens; adieu to the King of the Mountains!

I was about to leap to the bottom of the ravine, when a whitish form jumped up before me, and I heard the most furious barking which had ever awakened morning echoes. Alas! Monsieur, the enemies of man roamed at all hours around the camp, and one of them had scented me. I cannot describe the fury and hate which possessed me at meeting him; one does not detest to this degree an irrational being. I would have much preferred to find myself face to face with a wolf, with a tiger, or a white bear, noble beasts, who would have eaten me without saying anything, but who would not have denounced me. Ferocious beasts hunt for themselves; but to think of this horrible dog who was about to devour me, with a great uproar, in order to serve Hadgi-Stavros! I overwhelmed him with insults; I hurled the most odious names at him; do the best I could yet he spoke louder than I. I changed my tune, I tried the effect of kind words, I spoke to him sweetly in Greek, in the tongue of his fathers; he gave but one response to all my advances, and the response awoke the mountain echoes. A thought struck me! I was silent; he ceased barking. I stretched myself out among the pools of water; he crouched at the foot of the rock with low growls. I pretended to sleep; he slept. I glided, inch by inch, toward the brook; he was up with a bound, and I had only time to regain my platform. My hat remained in the hands of the enemy, or rather, in the teeth of the enemy. An instant afterward, it was no more than a pulp, a chewed up mass, a rag of a hat! Poor hat! I pitied it! I put myself in its place. If I could have escaped, less a few mouthfuls, I would not have considered the matter a great while, I would have made allowances for the dog's share. But these monsters are not satisfied with killing people, they eat them!

I was convinced that he was hungry; that if I could find enough to surfeit him, he might possibly bite me, but he would not devour me. I had some provisions, I would sacrifice them; my only regret was that I did not have a hundred times more. I threw a piece of bread to him; he swallowed it in one mouthful; imagine a pebble which falls into a well. As I looked piteously at the small portion which still remained, I saw, in the bottom of the box, a white package, which gave me a new idea. It was a small amount of arsenic, used in my zoological preparations. I used it in stuffing birds, but no law prevented me from putting a few grains into the body of a dog. My speaker, with sharpened appetite, demanded more: "Wait," I said to him, "I am going to give thee a morsel of my own making!" The package contained about 35 grammes of a pretty powder, white and shining. I turned five or six into a small pool of water, and I put the remainder in my pocket. I carefully diluted a portion for the animal; I waited until the acid was well dissolved; I dipped into the solution a piece of bread, which soaked it all up, like a sponge. The dog sprang upon it with a good appetite and swallowed it at once.

Why was not I provided with a little strychnine, or some other good poison more fearful than arsenic? It was after three o'clock, and the results of my experiment were not instantaneous. About half after three, the dog began to howl with all his strength. I had not gained much; barking and howling, cries of fury, or of agony, were all to the same purpose—that is—the awakening of Hadgi-Stavros. Soon the animal fell into frightful convulsions; he foamed at the mouth; he was seized with nausea, he made violent effort to throw off the poison. It was a sweet sight to me, and I enjoyed it; the death of the enemy was my only way of escape, and death was vanquishing him. I hoped that, conquered by the poison, he would permit me to leave; but he raged against me, he opened his foam-flecked and bloody jaws, as if to reproach me with my presents, and to tell me that he would not die without vengeance. I threw my handkerchief to him; he tore it as savagely as my hat. The sky began to lighten. I became convinced that I had committed a useless murder. An hour later, the brigands would be upon me. I looked up to that horrid place which I had left without expecting to return to it, and to which the dog's endurance was forcing me. A volume of water suddenly poured over the rock and threw me, face down. The icy water, filled with huge pieces of turf, stones, fragments of rock rolled over me. The dam had broken, and the whole body of water poured over my head. A trembling seized me! I became chilled, my blood congealed! I looked toward the dog; he was still at the foot of my rock, struggling with death, with the current, with anything, jaws open and eyes turned towards me. This must end. I took off my box, clutched it by the straps, and pounded that hideous head with such fury that the enemy left me the field of battle. The torrent seized him, rolled him over two or three times, and carried him, I know not where.

I jumped into the water; it was up to my waist; I clung to the rocks; I went with the current; I was over the bank; I shook myself, I cried: "Hurrah for Mary-Ann!"

Four brigands rose out of the earth! they caught me by the collar, saying: "Here thou art, assassin! Come! we will take thee back! the King will be happy! Vasile will be avenged!"

It appeared, that without knowing it, I had drowned my friend, Vasile.

At that time, Monsieur, I had never killed a man; Vasile was my first. I have fought others since, to defend myself and to save my life; but Vasile is the only one who has caused me any remorse, although his end was, probably, the result of a very innocent imprudence. You know that it is only the first step! No murderer, discovered by the police, surrounded with soldiers and led to the scene of his crime, hung his head more humbly than I. I dared not raise my eyes to the good people who had arrested me; I did not feel equal to encountering the eyes of these reprobates; I trembled; I presented a guilty appearance; I knew that I must appear before my judge, and be placed before my victim. How could I confront the King's frown, after what I had done? How could I see, without dying of shame, the inanimate body of the unfortunate Vasile? My knees shook; I would have fallen but for the kicks I received from those following me.

I crossed the deserted camp, the King's cabinet, occupied by some of the wounded, and I descended, or, rather, I fell to the bottom of the staircase to my chamber. The waters had receded, leaving traces of mud everywhere. A small pool of water still remained where I had raised the dam. The bandits, the King, and the monk, stood in a circle, about a dark and muddy object, the sight of which made my hair stand on end: it was Vasile! Heaven preserve you, Monsieur, from the sight of a corpse of your own making! The water and the mud, rushing over him, had deposited on him a hideous layer. Have you ever seen a great fly which had been caught, three or four days before, in a large spider-web? The artisan of the web, not being able to rid himself of his visitor, had enveloped him in a tangle of gray threads, and changed him to an unformed and unrecognizable mass. Such was Vasile a few hours after he had dined with me. I found him ten feet from the path where I had bidden him farewell. I do not know whether the brigands had laid him there, or whether he had thrown himself there, in his convulsions of agony; I am inclined to believe, however, that death had come to him gently. Full of wine as I had left him, he must have succumbed, without a struggle, to some cerebral congestion.

A menacing murmur, which was a bad augury, greeted my arrival. Hadgi-Stavros, with pale and contracted brow, walked up to me, seized me by the left wrist, and dragged me so violently that he dislocated my arm. He threw me into the middle of the circle with such force, that I almost fell on my victim; I instantly recoiled.

"Look!" he cried in thundering tones, "look at what you have done! rejoice in your work; gaze upon your crime! Wretch! but where would you have stopped? Who would have said, the day I received you here, that I had opened my door to an assassin?"

I stammered some excuses; I tried to show the judge that I was guilty only of imprudence. I warmly accused myself of having intoxicated my guardian in order to escape his watchfulness, and to flee without hindrance from my prison; but I defended myself from the crime of assassinating him. Was it my fault if the rise of waters drowned him an hour after my departure? The proof that I had wished him no evil, was that I had not stabbed him when he was dead drunk, and that I had his weapons at hand. They could wash the body and see that he was not wounded.

"At least," the King replied, "confess that your act was very selfish and very culpable! When your life was not threatened, when you were held here for only a small sum, you fled through avarice; you thought only of saving a few écus, and you did not trouble yourself about this poor unfortunate whom you left to die! You never thought of me! that you were going to deprive me of a valuable officer! And what moment did you choose to betray us? The day on which all kinds of troubles assailed us; when I had sustained a defeat; when I had lost my best soldiers; when Sophocles was wounded; when the Corfuan was dying; when the little Spiro, upon whom I relied, was killed; when all my men were weary and discouraged; it was then you had the heart to relieve me of Vasile! Have you, then, no humane sentiments? Would it not have been a hundred times better to have paid your ransom honestly, as became a good prisoner, than to have it said you sacrificed a life for 15,000 francs?"

"Eh! Zounds! You have killed people, and for less!"

He replied with dignity: "That is my business; it is not yours. I am a brigand, and you are a doctor. I am Greek, and you are German."

To that, I had nothing to reply. I felt convinced from the trembling of every fiber of my heart, that I had neither been born nor brought up to the profession of killing men. The King, angry at my silence, raised his voice, and said:

"Do you know, miserable young man, who was the excellent man of whose death you are guilty? He was a descendant of those heroic brigands of Souli who fought fierce battles for their religion, and against Ali de Tebelen, Pasha of Janina. For four generations, all of his ancestors have either been hung or decapitated; not one has died in his bed. Only six years ago, his own brother perished in Epirus, having been condemned to death; he had killed a Mohammedan. Devotion and courage are hereditary in that family. Never did Vasile forget his religious duties. He gave to the churches; he gave to the poor. At Easter, he always lighted a larger taper than any one else. He would have killed himself rather than violate the law of abstinence, or eat meat on a fast-day. He economized in order to retire to a convent on Mount Athos. Did you know it?"

"I humbly confessed that I did know it.

"Do you know that he was the most steadfast of all my band? I do not wish to detract from the personal merit of those who are listening to me, but Vasile possessed a blind devotion, a fearless obedience, a true zeal under all circumstances. No labor was too great for his courage; no occupation too repugnant for his fidelity. He would have killed every one in the kingdom if I had ordered him to do so. He would have torn out his best friend's eye, if I had given him a sign with my little finger. And you have killed him! Poor Vasile! when I shall have a village to burn, a miser to torture, a woman to cut in pieces, an infant to burn alive, who will replace thee?"

All the brigands, electrified by this funeral oration, cried in one voice. "We! We!" Some held out their arms to the King, others unsheathed their daggers; the most zealous leveled their pistols at me. Hadgi-Stavros checked their enthusiasm: he stepped in front of me to shield me, and went on with his discourse in these words:

"Be consoled, Vasile, thou shalt not rest without vengeance. If I listened only to my grief, I would offer to thy manes thy murderer's head; but it is worth 15,000 francs, and that thought restrains me. Thou, thyself, if thou couldst speak, as formerly in our councils, thou wouldst beg me to spare him; thou wouldst refuse so costly a vengeance. It is not proper, in the circumstances in which thy death has left us, to do foolish things, and to throw money away."

He stopped a moment; I drew a deep breath.

"But," the King went on, "I will know how to reconcile interest with justice. I will chastise the guilty one without risking the capital. His punishment shall be the most beautiful ornament of funeral obsequies; and, from above, from the homes of the Palikars, to which thy spirit has gone, thou shalt contemplate, with joy, an expiatory punishment, which shall not cost us a soul!"

This peroration aroused the audience. I was the only one not charmed. I puzzled my brain trying to imagine what the King had in store for me, and I felt so little assured, that my teeth chattered. Surely, I ought to esteem myself happy to save my life, and the preservation of my head seemed no mean advantage; but I knew the inventive imagination of these Greeks of the highway. Hadgi-Stavros, without putting me to death, could inflict such chastisement as would make me hate life. The old rascal refused to inform me as to what punishment he had in store for me. He pitied my agony so little, that he compelled me to assist in the funeral ceremonies of his lieutenant.

The body was stripped of its garments, carried to the brook, and bathed. Vasile's features were changed but little; his mouth, half-open, still bore the silly smile of the drunkard; his open eyes preserved a stupid look. His limbs had not lost their suppleness; the rigor mortis does not come, for a long time, to those who die by accident.

The King's coffee-bearer and pipe-bearer proceeded to dress the dead. The King bore the expenses as heir. Vasile had no relatives, and all his property reverted to the King. They clothed the body in a fine shirt, a shirt of beautiful percale, and a vest embroidered with silver. They covered his wet locks with a bonnet which was nearly new. They put leggins of red silk on the legs which would never run again. Slippers of Russia leather were slipped on his feet. In all his life, poor Vasile had never been so clean nor so gorgeous. They touched his lips with carmine; they whitened and rouged his face as if he was a young actor about to step on the stage. During the whole operation, the bandit orchestra executed a lugubrious air, which you must have heard in the streets of Athens. I congratulate myself that I did not die in Greece, because the music is abominable, and I never could have consoled myself, if I had been buried to that air.

Four brigands began to dig a grave in the middle of the chamber, upon the place where Mrs. Simons' tent stood, and on the spot where Mary-Ann had slept. Two others ran to the store-house to find wax-tapers, which they distributed. I was given one with all the others. The monk intoned the service for the dead. Hadgi-Stavros made the responses in firm tones which went to the depths of my soul. There was a light breeze, and the wax from my taper fell upon my hand in a burning shower; but that, alas! was a small thing in comparison with what awaited me. I would have willingly endured that trouble, if the ceremony could never have been finished.

It was finished at last. When the last oration had been delivered, the King solemnly approached the bier on which the body lay, and kissed Vasile's lips. The bandits, one by one, followed his example. I shivered at the thought that my turn was coming. I tried to hide behind two who had already performed their duty, but they saw me and said: "It is your turn! Start then! You certainly owe him that!"

Was this, at last, the expiation which awaited me? A just man would have been satisfied, at least. I swear to you, Monsieur, that it is no child's play to kiss the lips of a corpse, above all, when one can reproach one's self with being the instrument of his death. I walked toward the bier, I looked at the face whose eyes seemed to laugh at my embarrassment. I bent my head, I slightly touched the lips. A humorous brigand applied his hand to the nape of my neck. My mouth struck the cold lips! I felt the icy teeth, and seized with horror, I raised my head, carrying away with me I know not what terror of death, which seizes me at this moment! Women are very fortunate, they have the resource of fainting!

They then lowered the body into the earth, they threw in a handful of flowers, a loaf of bread, an apple, and a little wine. This latter was the thing of which he had the least need. The grave was quickly filled, more quickly than I wished. A brigand observed that they must get two sticks for a cross. Hadgi-Stavros replied: "Be quiet! we will put up milord's sticks." I leave it to you to think whether my heart beat tumultuously. What sticks? What was there in common between sticks and me?

The King made a sign to his pipe-bearer, who ran to the office and came back with two long laurel poles. Hadgi-Stavros took the funeral bier and laid it upon the grave. He pressed it down hard into the freshly turned earth, and he raised it up at one end, while the other lay in the soil, and he smilingly said to me: "It is for you that I am working! Take off your shoes, if you please!"

He must have read in my eyes a question full of agony and terror, for he replied to the demand which I dared not address to him:

"I am not wicked, and I have always detested useless severity. That is why I wish to inflict on you a chastisement which will be of use to us, inasmuch as it will dispense with any future watchfulness over you. You have had for several days a craze to escape. I hope, that when you have received twenty blows of the stick upon the soles of your feet, you will no longer need to be watched, and your love for traveling will cease for some time. I know what the punishment is; the Turks treated me to a dose of it in my youth, and I know, by experience, that one does not die of it. One suffers much from it; you will cry out, I warn you of it. Vasile will hear from the depths of his tomb, and he will be pleased with us."

At this announcement, my first thought was to use my legs while I still had the freedom to do so. But you must believe that my will was very weak, for it was impossible to put one foot before the other. Hadgi-Stavros raised me from the ground as lightly as we pick up an insect in our path. I felt myself bound down and unshod, before a thought, leaving my brain, had time to act upon any of my members. I knew neither upon what they supported my feet, nor how they kept them from falling at the first stroke of the stick. I saw the two sticks lifted in the air, the one to the right, the other to the left; I closed my eyes and waited. I certainly did not wait the tenth part of a second, and yet, so short a time was sufficient to send a tender thought to my father, a kiss to Mary-Ann, and more than a hundred imprecations to be divided between Mrs. Simons and John Harris.

I did not become unconscious for an instant; it is a weakness which I never possessed, I have told you so. There was, also, nothing to lose. The first blow was so terrific that I believed that those which followed could amount to little. It took me in the middle of the soles, under that small, elastic arch, just in front of the heel, which supports the body. It was not the foot that hurt me most that time; but I believed that the bones of my poor legs were breaking in pieces. The second blow struck lower, just under the heels; it gave me a shock, profound, violent, which made my whole vertebral column quiver, and filled my brain with a frightful tumult that almost split my cranium. The third was given directly on the toes and produced an acute and stinging sensation, which shot all over my body and made me believe, for an instant, that the stick had hit me on the end of the nose. It was at this moment that the blood flowed for the first time. The blows succeeded each other in the same order and in the same places, at equal intervals. I had enough courage to keep silent during the first two; I cried out at the third; I howled at the fourth; I groaned at the fifth, and those which followed. At the tenth, the flesh itself could suffer no more; I was silent. But the prostration of my physical force diminished, in no wise, the clearness of my perceptions. I could not have raised my eyelids, and yet the lightest sounds reached my ears. I lost no word of what was said around me. It was an observation which I shall remember later, if I practice medicine. Doctors do not hesitate to condemn a sick man, four feet from his bed, without thinking that perhaps the poor devil can hear them. I heard a young brigand say to the King: "He is dead. What good to weary two men without profit to any one?" Hadgi-Stavros replied: "Fear nothing. I received sixty, one after another, and two days afterward I danced the Romanique."

"How didst thou do that?"

"I used the pomade of the Italian renegade, Ludgi-Bey—Where were we? How many blows?"

"Seventeen."

"Three more, my children; and lay on the last ones hard."

The stick had done its work well. The last blows fell upon a bloody but insentient mass of flesh. Pain had nearly paralyzed me!

They raised me from the stretcher; they unbound the cords; they swathed my feet with compresses dipped in fresh water, and, as I had the thirst of the wounded, they gave me a large cup of wine. Anger returned with my strength. I do not know whether you have ever been bastinadoed, but I know nothing more humiliating than physical chastisement. In order to become the sovereign of the whole world, I would not, for an instant, be the slave of a vile stick. Born in the nineteenth century, understanding the use of steam and electricity, possessing a good share of the secrets of nature, knowing thoroughly all that science has invented for the well-being and security of man, knowing also how to cure fevers, how to prevent taking small-pox, and then, not to be able to defend one's self against a blow from a stick. It is a little too much, surely! If I had been a soldier and had submitted to corporal punishment, I should certainly have killed my chiefs!

When I felt myself seated on the slimy ground, my feet paralyzed with pain, my hand useless; when I saw around me the men who had beaten me, the ones who had struck me and those who had seen me punished;

anger, shame, a feeling of outraged dignity, of justice violated, of intelligence brutalized, swept through my enfeebled body in a wave of hate, of revolt, and of vengeance. I forgot everything, prudence, interest, discretion, the future, and I gave free vent to the thoughts which stifled me; a torrent of abuse poured from my lips, while an overflow of bile mounted to my eyes. Surely, I am no orator, and my solitary studies have given me no exercise in the use of words, but indignation, which has made some poets, lent me, for a quarter of an hour, the savage eloquence of those prisoners who rendered up their souls with insults and who breathed their last sighs in the face of the Roman conquerors. Everything which can outrage a man in his pride, in his affections, and in his dearest sentiments I said to the King of the Mountains. I put him in the rank with unclean animals, and I denied him even the name of man. I insulted him through his mother, his wife, his daughter, and all of his posterity. I would like to repeat to you, verbatim, all that I made him listen to, but words are wanting to-day, as I am not angry. I invented terms which are not found in the dictionary, but which were understood, however, for the audience of outcasts howled under my words like a pack of hounds under the lash of whippers-in. But although I kept watch of the old Palikar, eagerly scanning the muscles of his face, and searching for the slightest trace of a frown, I could discern not the slightest sign of emotion. Hadgi-Stavros' face was like that of a marble statue. He replied to all insults with a contemptuous silence.

His attitude exasperated me to madness. I was certainly insane for a moment. A red cloud like blood passed before my eyes. I rose suddenly on my wounded feet. I saw a pistol thrust in the waist-band of one of the brigands, I pulled it out, I aimed it at the King, I drew the trigger, and fell back murmuring, "I am avenged!"

It was the King himself who raised me. I looked at him with an astonishment as great as if I had seen him walking out of hell. He seemed not at all moved, and smiled as tranquilly as an immortal. And moreover, Monsieur, I had not missed him. My ball had touched his forehead, a little above the left eyebrow; a trace of blood testified to it. Possibly the pistol was badly loaded, or the powder poor, or it may be, that the ball had glanced across the bone, but whatever it was, my bullet had made only an abrasion.

The invulnerable monster seated me carefully on the ground, leaned toward me, pulled my ear and said: "Why do you attempt the impossible, young man? I warned you that I had a head that was bullet-proof, and you know that I never lie. Were you not told that Ibrahim had seven Egyptians shoot at me and that he was unsuccessful? I hope that you do not pretend to be more powerful than seven Egyptians? But do you know that you have a nimble hand for a Northern man? Peste! if my mother, of whom you spoke lightly a few moments ago, had not endowed me with strength, I would now be a dead man. Another, in my place, would have died without having time to say, 'Thank you!' As for me, such things rejuvenate me. It recalls my best days. At your age, I exposed my life four times a day, and I only digested the better for it. Come, I will pardon you your hasty action. But as all my subjects are not proof against bullets, and that you may commit no new imprudence, I shall apply to your hands the same treatment as your feet received. Nothing prevents us from punishing you immediately; I will wait, however, until to-morrow, in the interests of your health. You see the stick is a blunt weapon which kills no one; you have yourself proved that one bastinadoed man is worth two. To-morrow's ceremony will occupy you. Prisoners do not know how to pass the time. It was idleness which gave you bad counsels. Rest easy, moreover; as soon as your ransom arrives, I will cure your wounds. I still have some of Ludgi-Bey's balm. There will be no signs of them at the end of two days, and you can dance at the ball at the Palace, without telling your partners that they are leaning on the arm of a cavalier who has been beaten."

I am not a Greek, and the insults wounded me as grievously as the blows. I shook my fist in the old rascal's face, and cried out with all my strength:

"No, wretch! my ransom will never be paid! No! I have not asked anyone for the money! Thou wilt get from me only my head, which will serve thee nothing. Take it quickly if it seems good to thee. It will do me a favor and thyself also. Thou wilt spare me two weeks of torture, and the disgust of looking at thee, which is the most of all. Thou wilt save my board for fifteen days. Do not miss it, it is the only benefit that thou wilt reap from me!"

He smiled, shrugged his shoulders, and replied: "Ta! ta! ta! ta! Thus it is with young people! Extremists in everything! They throw the helve after the hatchet. If I listened to you, I would regret it before eight hours had passed, and so would you. The Englishwomen will pay, I am sure of it. I know women yet, although I have lived in retirement for a long time. What would be said if I killed you to-day, and your ransom arrived to-morrow? The story would go out that I had broken my word, and my prisoners would allow themselves to be killed like sheep, without asking a centime of their parents. It would spoil the trade."

"Ah! thou believest that the Englishwomen will pay thee, my clever fellow? Yes, they will pay thee as thou meritest!"

"You are very good."

"Their ransom will cost thee 80,000 francs, dost thou hear? Eighty thousand francs out of thy pocket!"

"Do not say such things. One would think that the blows of the stick had turned your brain."

"I tell thee the truth. Dost thou recall the name of thy prisoners?"

"No, but I have it in writing."

"I will jog thy memory. The lady called herself Mrs Simons."

"Well!"

"Partner of the firm of Barley in London."

"My banker?"

"Precisely."

"How doest thou know my banker's name?"

"Because thou didst dictate before me."

"What matter, after all? They cannot escape; they are not Greeks, they are English; the courts—I will make complaint!"

"And thou wouldst lose. They have a receipt!"

"That is so. But by what mischance did I give them a receipt?"

"Because I advised thee to do it, poor man!"

"Wretch! dog wrongly baptized! heretic of hell! thou hast ruined me! thou hast betrayed me! Thou hast robbed me! eighty thousand francs! I am responsible! If they were the bankers of the company, I would lose only my share. But they hold only my capital; I shall lose it all. Art thou very sure that she is a partner of the firm of Barley?"

"As I am sure of dying to-day."

"No! thou shalt not die till to-morrow. Thou hast not suffered enough. We will make thee pay for those 80,000 francs. What punishment can we invent? Eighty thousand francs! Eighty thousand deaths would be little. What have I done to this traitor who has robbed me! Peuh! Child's play, a pleasantry! He has not howled two hours! I must invent something better. But may be there are two firms of the same name?"

"Cavendish Square, No. 31."

"Yes, it is the same. Fool! why didst thou not warn me instead of betraying me? I would have asked double the sum. They would have paid it; they have the means. I would not have given the receipt; I will never give another. No! no! it is the last time! Received a hundred thousand francs of Mrs. Simons! What a foolish sentence! Was it really I who dictated that? But I reflect now; I did not sign it. Yes, but my seal is equal to a signature! There are twenty letters in my name. Why didst thou demand this receipt? What do you expect from those ladies? Fifteen thousand francs for thy ransom? Selfishness, everywhere! Thou shouldst have confided in me; I would have let thee go without the ransom; I would even have paid thee. If thou art poor, as thou sayest thou art, thou shouldst know how good money is. Thou thinkest only of a sum of 80,000 francs? Dost thou know what a heap that would make in a room? How many pieces of gold? How much money one could make in business with 80,000 francs? It is a calamity! Thou hast robbed me of a fortune! Thou hast robbed my daughter, the only being I love in the world. It is for her that I work. But, if thou knowest my affairs, thou knowest that I scour the mountains for a whole year to gain 40,000 francs. Thou hast plundered me of two years' income; it is as if I had slept for two years!"

I had then found the tender chord. The old Palikar was touched to the heart. I knew that there was a heavy score against me, and I expected no mercy, and moreover, I experienced an intense joy in seeing that impassable mask torn asunder and that stony face wrung with emotion. I rejoiced to see in his wrinkled face, the convulsive movements of passion, as the shipwrecked boat lost in a raging sea, admires, afar off, the wave which is to engulf it. I was like the thinking reed, which the brutal universe crushes into a shapeless mass, and which consoles itself in dying with the lofty thought of its superiority. I said to myself, with pride: "I shall die by torture, but I am the master of my master, and the executioner of my execution!"

VII.

JOHN HARRIS.

The King contemplated his vengeance, as a man who has fasted three days contemplates a bountiful repast. He examined, one by one, all the dishes, I mean to say all the tortures; he licked his dry lips, but he knew not where to commence nor what to choose. One would have said that excess of hunger spoiled his appetite. He struck his head with his fist, as if he could force out some ideas, but they came so rapidly that it was not easy to seize one in its passage. "Speak!" he cried to his subjects. "Advise me! What good are you, if you are not able to give me advice? Shall I await the coming of the Corfuan, or until Vasile shall speak from the depths of his tomb? Find for me, beasts that you are, some torture for the loss of 80,000 francs."

The young pipe-bearer said to his master: "An idea strikes me. Thou hast one officer dead, another absent, and a third wounded. Put up their places for competition. Promise us that those who shall tell of the best way to avenge thee, shall succeed Sophocles, the Corfuan, and Vasile."

Hadgi-Stavros smiled complacently at this stratagem. He stroked the young boy's chin and said to him:

"Thou art ambitious, my little man! All in good time! Ambition is the result of courage. Agreed, for a competition! It is a modern idea, a European idea, that pleases me. To reward thee, thou shalt give thy advice, first; and if thou findest something very good, Vasile shall have no other heir but thee."

"I would," said the child, "pull out some of my lord's teeth, put a bit in his mouth, and make him run, bridled, till he dropped from fatigue."

"His feet are too sore; he would fall down at the first step. And you others? Tambouris, Moustakas, Coltzida, Milotia, speak, I am listening."

"I," said Coltzida, "I would break boiling hot eggs under his arm-pits. I tried it on a woman of Magara, and I had much fun."

"I," said Tambouris, "I would put him on the ground with a rock weighing five hundred pounds on his chest. It thrusts out one's tongue and makes one spit blood; it is fine!"

"I," said Milotia, "I would put vinegar in his nostrils, and drive thorns under every nail. One sneezes violently and one does not know what to do with one's hands."

Moustakas was one of the cooks of the band. He proposed to cook me in front of a small fire. The King's face expanded.

The monk assisted at the conference, and let them talk without giving his advice. He, however, took pity on me, according to the measure of his sensibility, and helped me as far as his intelligence permitted. "Moustakas," he said, "is too wicked. One can torture milord finely without burning him alive. If you will give him salt meat without allowing him to drink he will live a long time, he will suffer a great deal, and the King will satisfy his vengeance without interfering with God's vengeance. It is my disinterested advice which I give you; I shall make nothing by it; but I wish everyone to be pleased, since the monastery has received its tithe."

"Halt, there!" interrupted the coffee-bearer. "Good old man, I have an idea which is better than thine. I condemn milord to die of hunger. The others will do any evil to him which pleases them; I will not hinder them. But I would place a sentinel before his mouth, and I would take care that he had neither a drop of water nor a crumb of bread. Weakness would redouble his hunger; his wounds would increase his thirst, and the tortures of the others would finally finish him to my profit. What dost thou say, Sire? Is it not well reasoned and will it not give me Vasile's place?"

"Go to the devil, all of you!" cried the King. "You would reason less calmly if the wretch had plundered you of 80,000 francs! Carry him away to the camp and take your pleasure out of him. But unhappy the one who kills him by any imprudence! This man must die only by my hand. I intend that he shall reimburse me, in pleasure, for all that he has taken from me in money. He shall shed his blood drop by drop, as a bad debtor who pays sou by sou."

You would not believe, Monsieur, with what struggles the most wretched man will cling to life. Truly, I longed to die; and the happiest thing which could happen to me would be to end it all with one blow.

Something, however, rejoiced me at Hadgi-Stavros' threat. I blessed the extension of my time. Hope sprang up in my heart. If a charitable friend had offered to blow out my brains I would have looked twice at him.

Four brigands took me by the shoulders and legs and carried me, a shrieking mass, to the King's cabinet. My voice awakened Sophocles on his pallet. He called his companions and made them tell him the news, and asked to look at me closely. It was the caprice of a sick person. They threw me down by his side.

"Milord," he said to me, "we are both very weak, but the odds are that I shall get well sooner than you do. It appears that they are already talking of my successor. How unjust men are! My place is up for competition. Oh, well! I wish to compete and to put myself in the race. You will bear witness in my favor and your groans will testify that Sophocles is not yet dead. You shall be bound, and I take upon myself the pleasure of tormenting you with one hand, as spiritedly as the strongest of the band."

In order to please the unfortunate fellow they bound me. He turned over towards me and began to pull out hairs, one by one, with the patience and the regularity of a professional hair remover. When I saw what this new punishment was to be, I believed that the wounded man, touched by my misery, and sympathizing with me because of his own sufferings, wished to shield me from his comrades, and give me an hour's respite. The extraction of one hair is not so painful, by a good deal, as the prick of a pin. The first twenty came out, one after the other, without any discomfiture. But soon I changed my tune. The scalp, irritated by a multitude of imperceptible lesions, became inflamed. A dull itching began on my head; it became a little livelier; and at last it was intolerable. I would like to have raised my hands to my head; I understood with what intuition the wretch had had me bound. Impatience but aggravated the trouble; all the blood in my body rushed to my head. Every time Sophocles approached his hand to my scalp, a woful shivering seized my whole body. A thousand inexplicable stingings tormented my arms and legs. The nervous system, irritated at every point, enveloped me in a network more exasperating than Dejanire's tunic. I rolled over on the ground, I groaned, I cried for mercy, I regretted the bastinado. The executioner had pity on me only when he had completely exhausted himself. When he felt his eyes become dim, his head heavy, and his arm weary, he made a last effort, plunged his hand into my hair, seized a fist full, and fell over on his pallet, drawing from me a despairing cry.

"Come with me," said Moustakas. "Thou shalt decide, in a corner by the fire, if I can compete with Sophocles, and whether I merit a lieutenancy."

He raised me like a feather and carried me to the camp, in front of a heap of resinous wood and piled up brushwood. He took off the bonds, he stripped me of my clothes, leaving me only my trousers. "Thou shalt be my under-cook," he said. "We will make the fire and we will prepare the King's dinner, together."

He lighted the stack of wood and laid me out on my back, about two feet from the mountain of flames. The wood crackled, the red cinders fell like hail around me. The heat became unbearable. I hitched along with my hands a little distance, but he came with a frying-pan in his hand, and pushed me back with his foot to the place where he had first laid me.

"Look well, and profit by my lessons. Here are the heart, liver, and kidneys from three sheep; there is enough to feed twenty men. The King will choose the most delicate morsels; he will distribute the remainder to his men. Thou wilt have none of it for the present, and if thou tastest my cooking, it will be with the eyes only."

I soon heard the bubbling in the sauce pan, and it reminded me that I had been fasting since the evening before. My hunger added one more torment. Moustakas held the pan under my eyes and made me look at the appetizing color of the meat. He thrust it under my nose and I smelled the steam of the food. Suddenly he perceived that he had forgotten the seasoning, and he hurried away to find the salt and pepper, leaving the sauce pan to my care. The first idea which came to me was to steal a piece of the meat, but the brigands were only ten feet away; they would stop me at once. "If I only had my package of arsenic," I thought. What could I have done with it? I had not put it back in my box. I thrust my hands into my pockets. I drew out a soiled paper and a handful of that beneficent powder, which would save me, perhaps, or at least avenge me.

Moustakas returned at the instant when I was holding my open hand above the sauce pan. He seized me by the arm, looked me straight in the eye, and said in a menacing tone: "I know what thou hast done."

I dropped my arm discouraged. The cook added:

"Yes, thou hast thrown something over the King's dinner."

"What?"

"A spell. But no matter. Believe me, my poor milord, Hadgi-Stavros is a greater sorcerer than thou art. I am going to serve his dinner. I will have my part of it, but thou shalt not taste it."

"Great good may it do thee!"

He left me before the fire, placing me in the care of a dozen brigands who were crunching black bread and bitter olives. These Spartans kept me company for an hour or two. They attended to my fire with the watchfulness of sick nurses. If, at times, I attempted to drag myself a little further away from my torture they cried out: "Take care, thou wilt freeze!" And they pushed me toward the flames with heavy blows of the burning brushwood. My back was covered with red spots, my skin was raised in blisters, my eyelashes had succumbed to the heat of the fire, my hair exhaled an odor of burning horn, and yet I rubbed my hands in glee at the thought of the King eating my cooking and that something startling would happen upon Parnassus before night.

Very soon Hadgi-Stavros' men re-appeared in the

camp, stomachs filled, eyes shining, faces smiling. "Go on!" I thought, "your joy and your health will soon fall like a mask, and you will curse each mouthful of the feast which I seasoned for you!" The celebrated poisoner, Locuste, must have passed some very pleasant moments during her life. When one has reason to hate men, it is pleasure enough to see a vigorous being who goes, who comes, who laughs, who sings, while carrying in his intestines a seed of death which will spring up and devour him. It is a little like the same joy a good doctor experiences at the sight of a dying man whom he is able to bring back to life. Locuste used medicine inversely, as I did.

My malevolent reflections were interrupted by a singular tumult. The dogs barked in chorus, and a messenger, out of breath, appeared on the plateau with the whole pack at his heels. It was Dimitri, the son of Christodule. Some stones thrown by the bandits freed him from his escort. He shouted at the top of his lungs: "The King! I must speak to the King!" When he was about twenty steps from us, I called to him in a doleful tone. He was terrified at the state in which he found me, and he cried out: "The fools! Poor girl!"

"My good Dimitri!" I said to him, "where dost thou come from? Will my ransom be paid?"

"The ransom is well at stake, but fear nothing, I bring good news. Good for you, bad for me, for him, for her, for everybody! I must see Hadgi-Stavros. There is not a moment to lose. Until I come back, suffer no one to do you any harm; she would die for it! You hear, you wretches; do not touch milord. For your life. The King would cut you in pieces. Conduct me to the King!"

The world is such that a man who speaks as a master is almost sure of being obeyed. There was so much authority in the voice of this servant, and his passion expressed itself in a tone so imperious that my guards, astonished and stupefied, forgot to keep me near the fire. I crept some distance away, and deliciously reposed upon the cold rock, until Hadgi-Stavros' arrival. He appeared not less agitated than Dimitri. He took me in his arms like a sick child, and carried me, without stopping, to that fatal chamber where Vasile was buried. He laid me on his own carpet with maternal solicitude; he stepped back and looked at me with a curious mixture of hate and pity. He said to Dimitri: "My child, this is the first time that I have left such a crime unpunished. He killed Vasile, that was nothing. He would have assassinated me, I pardoned him. But he robbed me, the scamp! Eighty thousand francs less in Photini's dowry! I sought for a punishment equal to his crime. Oh, rest easy! I should have found it. Unhappy that I am! Why did I not restrain my anger? I have treated him harshly. And she will bear the penalty. If she receives two blows of the stick upon her little feet I shall never see her again. Men do not die of it, but a woman, a child of fifteen!"

He cleared the place of all the men who were crowding around us. He gently unwound the bloody bandages which enveloped my wounds. He sent his pipe-bearer for the balm of Ludgi-Bey. He seated himself on the damp grass in front of me, he took my feet in his hands and looked at the wounds. An almost incredible thing to tell! There were tears in his eyes!

"Poor child!" he said, "you have suffered cruelly. Pardon me. I am an old brute, a wolf of the mountain, a Palikar. I was trained in ferocity from twenty years of age. But you see that my heart is good, since I regret what I have done. I am more unhappy than you, because your eyes are dry and I weep. I shall set you at liberty without a moment's delay, or rather, no, you cannot go away thus. I will cure you first. The balm is a sovereign remedy. I will care for you as for a son. Health shall return quickly. You must be able to walk to-morrow. She must not remain a day longer in your friend's hands. In the name of Heaven tell no one of our quarrel to-day! You know that I do not hate you! I have said so often. I sympathized with you and I gave you my confidence. I told you my most sacred secrets. Do you not remember that we were friends until Vasile's death? An instant's anger must not make you forget twelve days of good treatment. You would not wish to break a father's heart. You are an honest young man; your friend ought to be good like you."

"But who, then?"

"Who? That cursed Harris! that devilish American! that execrable pirate! that kidnapper of children! that assassin of young girls! that wretch whom I wish I held with you so that I could crush you in my hands, grind you together, and scatter your dust to the winds of my mountains! You are all the same, Europeans, a race of traitors, who dare not attack men, and who have courage to fight only against children. Read what he has written me and tell me if there are tortures cruel enough to chastise a crime like his!"

He savagely hurled a crumpled letter at me. I instantly recognized the writing, and I read:

"Sunday, May 11, on board The Fancy, Bay of Salamis.
"Hadgi-Stavros:
"Photini is on board under guard of four American cannons. I shall hold her as hostage as long as Hermann Schultz is prisoner. As thou treatest my friend, so shall I treat thy daughter. She shall pay hair for hair, tooth for tooth, head for head. Reply to me without delay, otherwise I shall come to see thee! John Harris."

On reading this letter I could not restrain my joy. "The good Harris!" I shouted, "I who accused him! But explain, Dimitri, why he has not rescued me sooner?"

"He has been away, Mr. Hermann; he was chasing pirates. He returned yesterday morning, unfortunately for us. Why did he not remain away!"

"Excellent Harris! He has not lost a single day. But where did he kidnap the daughter of this old scamp?"

"At our house, M. Hermann. You know her, Photini. You have dined more than once with her."

The Daughter of the King of the Mountains was then that boarding-school miss with the flat nose, who sighed for John Harris.

I concluded from this that the abduction had been accomplished without violence.

The pipe-bearer now came up with a package of linen and a bottle filled with yellow pomade. The King dressed my feet with practiced touch, and I experienced within an hour a certain relief. Hadgi-Stavros was, at this moment, a fine subject for the study of psychology. He had as much brutality in his eyes as delicacy in his touch. He unwound the bandages from my instep so gently that I scarcely felt it; but his glance said: "If I could only strangle thee!" He took out the pins as adroitly as a woman; but with what pleasure would he have thrust his cangiar into me.

When he had adjusted the bandages, he stretched out his clenched fists and savagely roared:

"I am no longer a King, since I must refrain from gratifying my anger! I, who have always commanded, I obey a threat! He, who has made millions of men tremble, is afraid! They will boast of it, without doubt; they will tell the whole world of it; Oh! for the means to silence those European gossips! They will publish it in their papers, perhaps even in their novels. Why did I marry? Ought such a man to have children? I was born to fight soldiers and not to rear up little girls! Thunder is not for children; cannons are not for children. If they were, they would no longer fear the thunder-bolts and cannon-balls. This John Harris may well laugh at me! What if I should declare war against him? What if I should capture his ship by force? I have attacked many, when I was a pirate, and twenty such cannons did not trouble me. But my daughter was not on board. Dear little one! You know her then, Monsieur Hermann? Why did you not tell me that you boarded with Christodule? I would have asked no ransom; I would have released you instantly, for love of Photini. Truly, I wish that she knew your language. She will be a princess in Germany, some day or other. Is it not true that she will make a beautiful Princess? I think so! Since you know her you will forbid your friend to do her any harm. Could you have the heart to see a tear fall from those dear eyes? She has never harmed you, the poor innocent! If anyone ought to expiate your sufferings, it is I. Tell M. John Harris that you bruised your feet on the paths; you may then do me any harm you choose."

Dimitri stopped this torrent of words. "It is very unfortunate that M. Hermann is wounded. Photini is not safe in the midst of those heretics, and I know M. Harris: he is capable of anything!"

The King scowled. Suspicions of a lover entered the father's heart. "Be off, then," he said to me; "I will carry you if necessary to the foot of the mountain; you can find, in some village, a horse, a carriage, a litter; I will furnish everything needed. But let him know, that from to-day, you are free, and swear to me, on the head of your mother, that you will tell no one of the injury which has been done you?"

I scarcely knew how I could endure the fatigues of the journey; but anything seemed preferable to the company of my tormentors. I feared that a new obstacle might arise before I was free. I said to the King: "Let us start! I swear to you by all I hold most sacred, that they shall not touch a hair of your daughter's head!"

He raised me in his arms, threw me over his shoulder, and mounted the staircase to his cabinet. The entire band rushed out in front of him and barred our passage. Moustakas, livid as a man attacked with cholera, said to him: "Where art thou going? The German has thrown a spell over the food. We are suffering all the pains of hell. We are frightfully ill, through his fault, and we wish to see him die."

My hopes were dashed to the ground. Dimitri's arrival; John Harris' providential interference; Hadgi-Stavros' change of front; the humiliation of that superb head to the feet of his prisoner; so many events, crowded into a quarter of an hour, had turned my head; I had already forgotten the past, and I had rashly begun to count on the future.

At the sight of Moustakas, I remembered the poison. I felt that any moment might precipitate a fearful event. I clung to the King of the Mountains, I wound my arms around his neck, I begged him to carry me away without delay. "It will redound to thy glory," I said to him. "Prove to these savages that thou art King! Do not reply! words are useless. Let us pass over their bodies. Thou knowest thyself what interest thou hast in saving me. Thy daughter loves John Harris; I am sure of it, she confessed it to me!"

"Wait!" he replied. "Let us pass first! we can talk later."

He laid me carefully down on the ground, and rushed, with clenched fists, into the midst of the bandits. "You are fools!" he shouted. "The first one who touches milord will answer to me. What spell do you say he has cast? I ate with you; am I ill? Let me pass! he is an honest man; he is my friend!"

Suddenly, he changed countenance; his legs gave way under the weight of his body. He seated himself near me, leaned toward me and said with more grief than anger:

"Imprudent! Why did you not tell me that you had poisoned us?"

I seized the King's hand; it was cold. His features were convulsed; his marble-like face became a frightful color. At this sight, my strength suddenly failed me, and I felt that I was dying. I had nothing more to hope for in the world; had I not condemned myself, in killing the only man who had any interest in saving me? My head fell on my breast, and I sat, helpless, by the side of the livid and shivering old man.

Moustakas and some of the others had, already, stretched out their hands to seize me and compel me to share their sufferings. Hadgi-Stavros had no strength to defend me. Occasionally, a terrible hiccough shook the King, as the wood-cutter's ax shakes an oak a hundred years old. The bandits were persuaded that he was dying, and that the invincible old man was about, at last, to be conquered by death. All the ties which bound them to their chief, bonds of interest, of fear, of hope, and of gratitude, broke like the threads of a spider's web. The Greeks are the most restive people in the world. Their inordinate and intemperate vanity was sometimes subdued, but like a steel ready to rebound. They knew how, in case of need, to lean upon the strongest, or how to modestly follow the lead of the ablest, but not how to pardon the master who had protected and enriched them. For thirty centuries or more, this nation has been composed of a people, egotistical and jealous, which only necessity has held together, which inclination separates, and which no human power could unite entirely.

Hadgi-Stavros learned to his cost that one does not command, with impunity, sixty Greeks. His authority did not survive an instant longer than his moral force or his physical vigor. Without mentioning the wounded men who shook their fists in our faces, while reproaching us for their sufferings, the able-bodied grouped themselves in front of their legitimate king, around a huge, brutal peasant, named Coltzida. He was the most garrulous and most shameless of the band, an impudent blockhead without talent and without courage; one of those who hide during action, and who carry the flag after a victory; but in like situations, fortune favors impudent braggarts. Coltzida, proud of his lungs, heaped insults, by the score, on Hadgi-Stavros, as a grave-digger heaps the earth on the grave of a dead man.

"Thou seest," he said, "a wise man, an invincible general, an all-powerful king, and invulnerable mortal! Thou hast not deserved thy glory, and we have been far-sighted in trusting ourselves to thee! What have we gained in thy company? How hast thou served us? Thou hast given us fifty-four miserable francs a month, a beggarly pittance. Thou hast fed us on black bread and mouldy cheese which you would not touch, while thou hast accumulated a fortune and sent ships loaded with gold to foreign bankers. What benefit have we received from our victories and for all the blood which we have shed in the mountains? Nothing! thou hast kept all for thyself, spoils, personal effects, prisoners' ransoms! It is true that thou hast left us the bayonet thrusts: it is the only profit of which thou hast not taken thy share. During the two years I have been with thee, I have received four wounds in the back, and thou hast not a scar to show! If, at least, thou hadst known how to lead us! If thou hadst chosen good opportunities, when there was little to risk and much to gain! Thou hast beaten us; thou hast been our executioner; thou hast sent us into the wolves' jaws! Thou hast then hastened to be done with us and to retire us on a pension! Thou wert longing so much to see us all buried near Vasile that thou deliveredst us to this cursed lord, who has thrown a spell over our bravest soldiers! But do not hope to cheat us from our vengeance. I know why thou wishest to have him go away; he has paid his ransom. But what dost thou wish to do with this money? Wilt thou carry it away to a foreign country? Thou art sick, opportunely, my poor Hadgi-Stavros. Milord has not spared thee, thou art dying also, and it is well! My friends, we are our own masters. We will no longer obey anyone, we will do whatever pleases us, we will eat the best, we will drink all of the wine of Aegina, we will burn an entire forest to cook whole herds, we will pillage the kingdom! we will take Athens and we will camp in the Palace gardens! You have only to allow yourselves to be led; I know the best methods! Let us begin by throwing the old man, with his much loved lord, into the ravine; I will then tell you what is necessary to do!"

Coltzida's eloquence came near costing us our lives, because his audience applauded. Hadgi-Stavros' old comrades, ten or a dozen devoted Palikars, who might have come to his aid, had eaten dessert at his table: they were also writhing in agony. But a popular orator cannot elevate himself above his fellows without creating jealousies. When it became clear that Coltzida proposed to become chief of the band, Tambouris and some other ambitious ones faced about and ranged themselves on our side. To a man they liked better the man who knew how to lead them than this insolent braggart, whose incapacity repelled them. They urged that the King had not long to live, and that he would appoint his successor from among the faithful who remained around him. It was no ordinary affair. The odds were that the capitalists would more readily ratify Hadgi-Stavros' choice, than endorse a revolutionary election. Eight or ten voices were raised in our defense. Ours, because our interests were one. I clung to the King of the Mountains, and he had one arm around my neck. Tambouris and his fellows put their heads together; a plan of defense was formed;

three men profited by the uproar to run, with Dimitri, to the arsenal, to get arms and cartridges, and to lay along the path a train of powder. They came back and discreetly mixed with the crowd. They formed into two parties; insults were hurled from one to the other. Our champions, with their backs to Mary-Ann's chamber, guarded the stair-case, they made a rampart of their bodies for us, and kept the enemy in the King's cabinet. In the scrimmage, a pistol-shot rung out. A ribbon of fire ran over the ground and the rock flew up with a fearful noise.

Coltzida and his followers, surprised by the detonation, ran to the arsenal. Tambouris lost not an instant; he raised Hadgi-Stavros, descended the stair-case in two bounds, laid him in a safe place, returned, picked me up, carried, and laid me at the King's feet. Our friends intrenched themselves in the chamber, cut trees, barricaded the stair-case, and organized a defense before Coltzida could return.

Then, we counted our forces. Our army was composed of the King, his two servants, Tambouris with eight brigands, Dimitri, and myself; in all fourteen men, of whom three were disabled. The coffee-bearer had been poisoned also, and he began to show the first rigors of illness. But we had two guns apiece, and a great supply of cartridges, while the enemy had no arms nor ammunition except what they carried on their persons. They possessed the advantage of numbers and point of vantage. We did not know exactly how many able-bodied men they had, but we must expect to meet twenty-five or thirty assailants. I need not describe to you the place of siege: you know it. Believe, however, that the aspect of the place had changed a great deal since the day when I breakfasted there for the first time, under guard of the Corfuan, with Mrs. Simons and Mary-Ann. The roots of our beautiful trees were exposed, and the nightingale was far away. What is more important for you to know, is, that we were protected on the right and left by rocks, inaccessible even to the enemy. They could attack us from the King's cabinet, and they could watch us from the bottom of the ravine. On the one hand, their balls flew over us; on the other, ours flew over the sentinels, but at such long range that it was wasting our ammunition.

If Coltzida and his companions had possessed the least idea of war, they could have done for us. They could have raised the barricade, entered by force, driven us into a corner, or thrown us over into the ravine. But the imbecile, who had two men to our one, thought to husband his ammunition, and place, as sharp-shooters, twenty stupid men who did not know how to discharge a gun. Our men were not much more skillful. Better commanded, however, and wiser, they managed to smash five heads before night fell. The combatants knew each other by name. They called to each other after the fashion of Homer's heroes. One attempted to convert the other by aiming at his cheek; the other replied by a ball and by argument. The combat was only an armed discussion when, from time to time, the muskets spoke.

As for me, stretched out in a corner, sheltered from

the balls, I tried to undo my fatal work, and to recall the poor King of the Mountains to life. He suffered cruelly; he complained of great thirst, and a sharp pain in the upper part of the abdomen. His icy hands and feet were violently convulsed. The pulse was irregular, the respiration labored. His stomach seemed to struggle against an internal execution, without being able to expel it. His mind had lost nothing of its vigor and its quickness; his bright and keen eye searched the horizon in the direction of the Bay of Salamis, and Photini's floating prison.

He grasped my hand and said: "Cure me, my dear child! You are a doctor, you ought to cure me. I will not reproach you with what you have done; you were right; you had reason to kill me, because I swore that without your friend Harris I would not have allowed you to escape me. Is there nothing to quench the fire which consumes me? I care nothing for life; I have lived long enough; but if I die, they will kill you, and my poor Photini will be sacrificed. I suffer! Feel my hands; it seems to me that they are already dead. Do you believe that this American will have the heart to carry out his threats? What was it you told me a little while ago? Photini loves him! Poor little one! I have brought her up to become the wife of a king. I would rather see her dead, than— no, I would rather, after all, that she should love this young man; perhaps he may take pity on her. What are you to him? a friend; nothing more; you are not even a compatriot. One may have as many friends as one wishes; one cannot find two women like Photini; I would strangle all my friends if I found it to my advantage; I would never kill a woman who loved me. If only he knew how rich she is! Americans are practical, at least, so it is said. But the poor, little innocent knows nothing about her fortune. I ought to have told her. But how can I let him know that she will have a dowry of four millions? We are Coltzida's prisoners. Cure me then, and by all the saints in paradise I will crush the reptile!"

I am not a physician, and all I know about toxicology is in its elementary treatment; I remembered, however, that arsenical poisoning was cured only by a method similar to "Doctor Sangrado." I used means to make the old man eject the contents of his stomach, and I soon began to hope that the poison was almost expelled. Reaction followed; his skin became burning hot, the pulse quickened, his face flushed, his eyes were blood-shot. I asked him if any one of his men knew enough to bleed him. He tied a bandage tightly around his arm, and coolly opened a vein himself, to the noise of the fusilade and while the bullets dashed around him. He let out a sufficient amount of blood, and asked me in a sweet and tranquil tone, what else there was to do. I ordered him to drink, to drink more, to keep on drinking, until the last particle of arsenic had been disposed of. The goat-skin of white wine which had killed Vasile was still in the chamber. This wine, mixed with water, brought back life to the King. He obeyed me like a child. I believe that the first time I held out the cup to him, his poor, old suffering Highness seized my hand to kiss it.

Toward ten o'clock he became much better, but his pipe-bearer was dead. The poor devil could neither rid himself of the poison, nor revive. They threw him into the ravine, at the top of the cascade. All our defenders were in good condition, without a wound, but famished as wolves in December. As for me, I had been without food for twenty-four hours, and I was very hungry. The enemy, in order to defy us, passed the night eating and drinking above our heads. They threw to us some mutton bones and some empty goat-skin bottles. Our men replied with some shots, guessing at the position of our foes. We could plainly hear the cries of joy and the groans of the dying. Coltzida was drunk; the wounded and the sick howled in unison; Moustakas did not shout for a long time. The tumult kept me awake the entire night near the old King. Ah! Monsieur, how long the nights seem to him who is not sure of the next day!

Tuesday morning broke gray and wet. The sky looked threatening at sunrise, and a disagreeable rain fell alike on friend and foe. But if we were wide awake enough to protect our arms and ammunition, General Coltzida's army had not taken the same precaution. The first engagement redounded entirely to our honor. The enemy was badly hidden, and fired their pistols with shaking hands. The game seemed so good a one, that I took a gun like the others. What happened I will write to you about at some future time, if I ever become a doctor. I have already confessed to murders enough for a man whose business it is not. Hadgi-Stavros followed my example; but his hands refused to act; his extremities were swollen and painful, and I announced to him, with my usual frankness, that this incapacity might last as long as he did.

About nine o'clock the enemy, who seemed to be very attentive in responding to us, suddenly turned their backs. I heard heavy firing which was not directed to us, and I concluded that Master Coltzida had allowed himself to be surprised in the rear. Who was the unknown ally who was serving us so good a turn? Was it prudent to effect a junction and to demolish our barricade? I asked nothing else, but the King believed that it was a troop of the line, and Tambouris gnawed his moustache. All our doubts were soon removed. A voice which was not unknown to me, cried: "All right!" Three young men, armed to the teeth, sprang forward like tigers, broke down the barricade and fell in our midst. Harris and Lobster held in each hand a six-shooter. Giacomo brandished a musket, the butt-end in the air, like a club: it was thus that he knew how to use fire-arms.

A thunder-bolt falling into the chamber would have produced less magical effect than the appearance of these men, who shot right and left, and who seemed to carry death in their hands. My three fellow-boarders, excited by the noise, elated with victory, perceived neither Hadgi-Stavros nor me. They only turned around in order to kill a man, and God knows! they did their work well. Our poor champions, astonished, affrighted, were overcome without having had time to defend themselves or to be recognized. I, who would have saved their lives, shouted from my corner; but my voice was drowned in the whistling of bullets, and the shouts of the conquerors. Dimitri, crouching between the King and me, vainly joined his voice to mine. Harris, Lobster, and Giacomo fired, ran here and there, knocked down, counting the blows, each in his own tongue.

"One!" said Lobster.

"Two!" responded Harris.

"Tre! quatro! cinque!" growled Giacomo. The fifth was Tambouris. His head split under the blow like a fresh nut struck by a stone. The brains were scattered about, and the body sunk into the water like a bundle of clothes which a washerwoman throws in the edge of a brook. My friends were a fine sight in their horrible work. They killed with ferocity, they delighted in the justice they meted out. While running toward the camp, the wind had blown away their hats; their locks were disheveled; their glistening eyes shone so murderously, that it was difficult to decide whether death was dealt by their looks or by their hands. One could have said that destruction was incarnate in this panting trio. When they had removed all obstacles from their path and they saw no enemies but the three or four wounded men stretched on the ground, they stopped to breathe. Harris' first thought was for me. Giacomo had only one care: he wished to ascertain whether, among the number, he had broken Hadgi-Stavros' head. Harris shouted: "Hermann, where are you?"

"Here!" I replied: and the three fighters ran at my call.

The King of the Mountains, feeble as he was, put one hand on my shoulder, raised himself from the rock, looked fixedly at these men who had killed such a number to reach him, and said in a firm tone: "I am Hadgi-Stavros!"

You know that my friends had waited for a long time for occasion to chastise the old Palikar. They had promised themselves to celebrate his death as a festival. They would avenge Mistra's little daughters; a thousand other victims; me, and themselves. But, however, I had no need to restrain them. There was such remains of greatness in this hero in ruins, that their anger fell from them and gave way to astonishment. They were all three young men, and at the age when one no longer takes arms against a disarmed enemy. I related to them, in a few words, how the King had defended me against his whole band, almost dead as he was, and on the same day on which I had poisoned him. I explained to them about the battle they had interrupted, the barricades they had broken down, and that strange contest in which they had interfered and killed our defenders.

"So much the worse for them!" said John Harris. We wear, like Justice, a bandage over our eyes. If the rogues performed a good deed before they died, it will be counted in their favor up above; I do not object to it."

"As for the men of whom we have deprived you, do not worry about them," said Lobster. "With two revolvers in our hands and two more in our pockets, we have each been worth twenty-four men. We have killed these; the others have only to come back. Is it not so, Giacomo?"

"As for me, I could knock down an army of bulls!" said the Maltese; "I am in the humor for it. And to think that one is reduced to sealing letters with two such fists as these!"

The enemy, however, recovered from their astonishment, had again begun the siege. Three or four brigands had poked their noses over our ramparts and saw the carnage. Coltzida knew not what to think of the three scourges who had struck blindly, right and left, among friends and foes; but he decided that either sword or poison must have freed the King of the Mountains. He prudently ordered the men to demolish our defense. We were out of sight, sheltered by the wall, about ten steps from the stair-case. The noise of the falling barricade warned my friends to reload their revolvers. The King allowed them to do so. He said to John Harris:

"Where is Photini?"

"On my ship."

"You have not harmed her?"

"Do you think that I have taken lessons from you in torturing young girls?"

"You are right, I am a miserable old dog; pardon me! Promise me to forgive her!"

"What the devil do you want me to do with her? Now that I have found Hermann, I will send her back to you whenever you wish."

"Without ransom?"

"You old beast!"

"You shall see whether I am an old beast!"

He passed his left arm around Dimitri's neck, he extended his shriveled and trembling hand toward the hilt of his sword, painfully drew the blade from the scabbard, and marched toward the stair-case where Coltzida and his men stood hesitating. They recoiled at sight of him, as if the earth had opened to allow the passage of the ruler of the infernal regions. There were fifteen or twenty, all armed; not one dared to defend himself, to make excuses, nor even to attempt to escape. They trembled in all their limbs, at sight of the terrible face of the resuscitated King. Hadgi-Stavros marched straight to Coltzida, who, paler and more horrified than the others, attempted to hide behind his companions. The King threw his arm backwards by an effort impossible to describe, and with one blow severed his head from his body. Instantly, a trembling seized him. His sword fell on the dead man and he did not deign to pick it up.

"Let us go on," he said, "I carry an empty scabbard. The blade is no longer of use, neither am I; I am done for!"

His old companions approached to ask pardon. Some of them begged him not to abandon them; they knew not what to do without him. He did not honor them with a word of response. He implored us to accompany him to Castia to find horses, and to Salamis to search for Photini.

The brigands allowed us to depart without hindrance. After a few steps, my friends noticed that I could scarcely step; Giacomo helped me along; Harris asked if I was wounded. The King gave me a beseeching look, poor man! I told my friends that I had attempted a perilous escape, and that my feet had been badly wounded. We carefully picked our way down the mountain paths. The groans of the wounded, and the voices of the bandits who were discussing matters, followed us for quite a distance. As we approached the village, the weather changed, and the path began to dry under our feet. The first ray of sunlight which burst forth seemed to me very beautiful. Hadgi-Stavros paid little attention to the outside world; he communed within himself. It is something to break off a habit of fifty years standing.

On the outskirts of Castia, we met the monk who was carrying a swarm of bees in a sack. He greeted us courteously, and excused himself for not having visited us since the evening before. The musket shots had intimidated him. The King saluted him and passed on. My friends' horses were waiting, with their guide, near the fountain. I asked them how they happened to have four horses. They said that M. Mérinay made one of the party, but that he had alighted to inspect a curious stone, and that he had not yet reappeared.

Giacomo Fondi lifted me to the saddle at arm's length; he could not resist the temptation. The King, assisted by Dimitri, painfully climbed into his. Harris and his nephew vaulted into theirs; Giacomo, Dimitri, and the guide preceded us on foot.

The path widening, I rode up beside Harris, and he

related to me how the King's daughter had fallen into his hands:

"Imagine;" he said to me. "I had just arrived from my cruise, much pleased with myself, and very proud of having run down a half-dozen pirates. I anchored off Piraeus, Sunday, at six o'clock; I landed; and as I had been eight days tête-à-tête with my head officer, I promised myself a little pleasure in conversation. I stopped a fiacre, I hired it for the evening. I arrived at Christodule's house in the midst of a general hubbub; I would never have believed that so much trouble could be found in a pastry-cook's house. Every one was there for supper. Christodule, Maroula, Dimitri, Giacomo, William, M. Mérinay and the little Sunday girl, more tricked out than ever. William related to me your story. It is useless to tell you that I made a great uproar. I was furious with myself for not having been in the city. My nephew assured me that he had done all he could. He had scoured the city for fifteen thousand francs, but his parents had opened only a limited credit for him; briefly, he had not found the amount. In despair, he addressed himself to M. Mérinay: but the sweet Mérinay pretended that all his money was lent to his intimate friends, far from here, very far;—farther than the end of the world!

"'Eh! Zounds!' I said to Lobster, 'it is in lead-money that one must pay the old scoundrel. For what good is it to be as dextrous as Nimrod, if one's talent is good only to break Socrates' prison? We must organize a hunt for the old Palikars! Once, I refused a journey to Central Africa: I have since regretted it. It is double pleasure to shoot an animal which defends itself. Provide plenty of powder and balls, and to-morrow morning we will set out on a campaign.' William took the bait, Giacomo brought his fist down in a crashing blow on the table; you know what Giacomo's fist-blows are. He swore that he would accompany us, provided he could find a single-barreled gun. But the most enraged of all was M. Mérinay. He wished to bathe his hands in the blood of those wretches. We accepted his services, but I offered to buy the game which he would bring back. He swelled out his little voice in the most comical fashion, and showing his fists to Mademoiselle, said that Hadgi-Stavros would have business to settle with him.

"I laughed gleefully like those who are always gay the night before a battle. Lobster became very merry at the thought of showing the bandits the progress he had made. Giacomo could not contain himself for joy; the corners of his mouth went around dangerously near his ears; he cracked nuts with the face of a nut-cracker of Nuremburg. M. Mérinay had a halo around his head. He was no longer a man, but a pyrotechnic display.

"Except us, the guests resembled alder trees. The pastry-cook's huge wife made signs of the cross; Dimitri raised his eyes to heaven, Christodule advised us to think twice before we provoked the King of the Mountains. But the girl with the flat nose, the one to whom you gave the name of Crinolina invariabilis, was plunged in grief which was quite amusing. She fetched great sighs like a wood-splitter; she did this only to keep herself in countenance, and I could have put in my left eye all the supper which she put into her mouth."

"She is a good girl, Harris."

"Good girl as much as you wish, but I find that your indulgence for her passes all bounds. I have never been able to pardon her for her dresses which thrust themselves obstinately under the legs of my chair, the odor of patchouli which she spreads around me, and the lackadaisical glances which she passes around the table. One would say, upon my word, that she is not capable of looking at a carafe without casting sheep's eyes at it. But if you love her, such as she is, there is nothing to be said. She left at nine o'clock for her boarding-school; I wished her bon voyage. Ten minutes afterward I shook hands with our friends, we made a rendezvous for the next day, I went out, I wakened my coachman and guess whom I found in my carriage? Crinolina invariabilis with the pastry-cook's servant.

"She placed her finger on her lips. I entered without saying a word, and we started. 'Monsieur Harris,' she said in very good English, by my faith, 'swear to me to renounce your plans against the King of the Mountains.'

"I began to laugh, and she began to weep. She declared that I would be killed; I replied that it was I who would kill the others; she objected to having Hadgi-Stavros killed; I wished to know why; at last, at the end of her eloquence, she cried out, as if in the fifth act of a play: 'He is my father!' Upon that I began to seriously reflect; once in a way does not count. I thought that it might be possible to recover a lost friend without risking two or three others, and I said to the young Palikar:

" 'Your father loves you?'

" 'More than his life.'

" 'He never refuses you anything?'

" 'Nothing that is necessary.'

" 'And if you should write to him that you wanted M. Hermann Schultz would he send him to you with the message-bearer?'

" 'No.'

" 'You are absolutely sure of it?'

" 'Absolutely.'

" 'Then, Mademoiselle, I have but one thing to do. Set a thief to catch a thief. I will carry you on board The Fancy, and I will hold you as a hostage until Hermann is returned.'

" 'I was about to propose it to you,' she said. 'At that price papa will send back your friend.' "

Here I interrupted John Harris' story.

"Oh, well! you do not admire the poor, young girl who loves you enough to give herself into your hands?"

"A fine affair!" he replied. "She wished to save that honest man, her father, and she well knew that once war was declared we would not let him escape. I promised to treat her with all the respect a gallant man ought to treat a woman. She wept until we reached Piraeus. I consoled her as best I could. She murmured: 'I am a lost girl!' I demonstrated to her by 'A' plus 'B' that she would find herself again. I made her get out of the carriage. I helped her and the servant into my boat, which now awaits us below. I wrote to the old brigand an explicit letter, and I sent an old woman with a little message to Dimitri.

"Since that time the beautiful weeper enjoys undisputed possession of my apartments. Orders were given that she was to be treated like the daughter of a king. I waited until Monday evening for her father's response; then my patience failed me; I returned to my first plan; I took my pistols; I notified my friends, and you know the rest. Now it is your turn; you ought to have a whole volume to recount."

"I must first speak to the King."

I approached him and said to him in a low tone: "I do not know why I told you that Photini was in love with John Harris. Fear must have turned my head. I have been talking with him, and I swear to you, on the head of my father, that she is as indifferent to him as if he had never spoken to her."

The old man thanked me with a motion of the hand, and I went back to John Harris, and related my adventures with Mary-Ann. "Bravo!" he exclaimed. "I find that the romance is not complete on account of the absence of a little love. A sufficient amount will do no harm."

"Excuse me," I answered. "There is no love in it at all! A firm friendship on one side, a little gratitude on the other. But nothing more is necessary, I think, to make a reasonably suitable marriage."

"Marry, my friend, and permit me to be a witness to your happiness."

"You have well earned it, John Harris."

"When shall you see her again? I would give much to be present at the interview."

"I would like to surprise her and meet her by chance."

"That is a good idea! After to-morrow, at the Court Ball! You are invited. I am, too. Your note lies on your table, at Christodule's house. Until then, my boy, you must remain on board my ship in order to recuperate a little. Your hair is scorched and your feet are wounded; we will have time to remedy all that."

It was six o'clock in the evening when the boat belonging to Harris put off to The Fancy. They carried the King on deck; he could not walk. Photini, weeping, threw herself into his arms. It was happiness to see that those whom she loved had survived the battle, but she found her father grown twenty years older. Possibly, also, she suffered from Harris' indifference. He delivered her to her father in a characteristic American fashion, saying: "We are quits! You have returned my friend to me; I have restored Mademoiselle to you. An even exchange is no robbery! Short accounts make long friends! And now, most venerable old man, under what beneficent region of the earth will you search for the one who is to hang you?"

"Pardon me," he replied, with a certain hauteur. "I have bidden adieu to brigandage forever. What would

I do in the mountains? All of my men are dead, wounded or scattered. I could form another band; but these hands which have been so powerful, refuse to act. Younger men must take my place; but I defy them to equal my fortune and my renown. What shall I do with what few years are left to me? I know not yet; but you may be sure that my last days will not be idle ones. I have to establish my daughter to dictate my memoirs. Possibly, even, if the shocks of this week have not wearied my brain too severely, I will consecrate to the service of the State my talents and my experience. May God give me health and strength! before six months have passed I shall be President of the Ministry!"

VIII.

THE COURT BALL.

Thursday, May 15, at six o'clock in the evening, John Harris, in full uniform, took me to Christodule's house. The pastry-cook and his wife gave me a warm reception, not without many sighs on account of the King of the Mountains. As for me, I embraced them heartily. I was happy in being alive, and I saw only friends on all sides. My feet were cured; my hair trimmed, my stomach full. Dimitri assured me that Mrs. Simons, her daughter, and her brother were invited to the Court Ball, and that the laundress had taken a dress to the Hotel des Etrangers. I enjoyed, in advance, Mary-Ann's surprise and joy. Christodule offered me a glass of Santorin wine. In this glorious beverage I thought to drink to liberty, riches, happiness. I mounted the staircase to my room, but before retiring I knocked at M. Mérinay's door. He received me in the midst of a medley of books and papers. "Dear sir, you see a man overwhelmed with work," he said. "I found, above the village of Castia, an antique inscription, which deprived me of the pleasure of fighting for you, and which for six days has puzzled me. It is absolutely unknown, I assure you of that. No one has seen it; I have the honor of discovering it; I intend to give it my name. The stone is a small monument of shelly limestone, 35 centimetres in height by 22, and set, by chance, on the edge of the path. The characters are of the finest period of art and cut to perfection. Here is the inscription as I copied it in my note-book:

"S. T. X. X. I. I.

"M. D. C. C. C. L. I.

"If I can translate it my fortune is made. I shall be made member of the Academy of Inscriptions and Belles-lettres of Pont-Audemer! But the task is a long and difficult one. Antiquity guards its secrets with jealous care. I greatly fear that I have come across a monument relative to the Eleusinian mysteries. In that case there may perhaps be two interpretations to discover; the one the vulgar or demontique; the other the sacred or hieratique. You must give me your advice."

I replied: "My advice is that of an ignorant man. I think that you have discovered a mile-stone such as one often sees on long roads, and that the inscription which has given you so much trouble can, without doubt, be translated thus:

"Stade, 22, 1851. Good evening, my dear M. Mérinay; I am going to write to my father and then put on my red uniform."

My letter to my parent was an ode, a hymn, a chant of happiness. The exuberant joy which filled my heart overflowed upon the paper. I invited the family to my wedding, not forgetting good Aunt Rosenthaler. I implored my father to sell his inn at once; I ordered that Frantz and Jean Nicolas should leave the service; I advised my other brothers to change their business. I took everything upon myself; I assumed the responsibility of the future of the whole family. Without losing a moment I sealed the letter and sent it by special messenger to Piraeus, to catch the German-Lloyd steamer, which sailed Friday morning at 6 o'clock. "In this way," I said to myself, "they will rejoice in my happiness almost as soon as I shall."

At a quarter to nine sharp I entered the Palace with John Harris. Neither Lobster, M. Mérinay nor Giacomo were invited. My three-cornered hat was a little rusty, but by candlelight this little defect was not noticeable. My sword was seven or eight centimetres too short; but what of that? Courage is not measured by the length of a sword, and I had without vanity the right to pass for a hero. The red coat was tight-fitting; it pinched me under the arms, and the trimming on the cuffs was quite a distance from my hands; but the embroidery showed to advantage, as papa had prophesied.

The ballroom, decorated with taste and brilliantly lighted, was divided into two sections. On one side behind the throne for the King and Queen were the fauteuils reserved for the ladies; on the other were chairs for the ugly sex. With one glance I swept the space occupied by the ladies. Mary-Ann had not yet arrived.

At nine o'clock I saw enter the King and Queen, followed by the Grand Mistress, the Marshal of the Palace, the aides-de-camp, the Ladies of Honor, and the orderly officers, among whom I recognized M. George-Micrommatis. The King was magnificently dressed in Palikar uniform, and the Queen was resplendent with exquisite elegancies which could come only from Paris. The gorgeousness of the toilets and the glitter of the national costumes made me almost forget Mary-Ann. I fixed my eyes on the door and waited.

The members of the Diplomatic Corps and the most distinguished guests were ranged in a circle around the King and Queen, who conversed pleasantly with those near them for a half hour or so. I was on the outside row with John Harris. An officer, standing in front of us, stepped back suddenly with his whole weight upon my foot and the pain drew from me an exclamation. He turned his head and I recognized Captain Pericles, freshly decorated with the Ordre du Sauveur. He made excuses and asked for news. I could not refrain from informing him that my health did not concern him. Harris, who knew my history entirely, politely said to the captain: "Is it not M. Pericles to whom I have the honor of speaking?"

"Himself!"

"I am charmed! Will you be good enough to accompany me, for a moment, into the card-room? It is still empty and we will be alone."

"At your orders, Monsieur."

M. Pericles, pale as a soldier who is leaving a hospital, smilingly followed us. Arrived, he faced John Harris and said to him: "Monsieur, I await your pleasure."

In reply Harris tore off his cross with its new ribbon, and put it in his pocket, saying: "There, Monsieur, that is all I have to say to you!"

"Monsieur!" cried the captain, stepping back.

"No noise, Monsieur, I pray you. If you care for this toy you can send two of your friends for it to Mr. John Harris, Commander of The Fancy."

"Monsieur," Pericles replied, "I do not know by what right you take from me a cross which is worth fifteen francs, and which I shall be obliged to replace at my own expense."

"Do not let that trouble you, Monsieur; here is an English sovereign, with the head of the Queen of England on it; fifteen francs for the cross, ten for the ribbon. If there is anything left, I beg of you to drink to my health."

"Monsieur," said the officer, pocketing the piece, "I have only to thank you." He saluted without another word, but his eyes promised nothing pleasant.

"My dear Hermann," Harris said to me, "it will be prudent for you to leave this country as soon as possible with your future bride. This gendarme has the air of a polished brigand. As for me, I shall remain here eight days in order to give him time to demand satisfaction. After that I shall obey the orders which I have received to go to the Sea of Japan."

"I am sorry that your ardor has carried you so far. I do not wish to leave Greece without a specimen or two of the Boryana variabilis. I have an incomplete one without the roots in my tin box which I forgot when we left the camp."

"Leave a sketch of your plant with Lobster or Giacomo. They will make a pilgrimage into the mountains for your sake. But for God's sake! make haste to get to a place of safety!"

In the meantime my happiness had not arrived at the ball, and I tired my eyes staring at all the dancers. Toward midnight I lost all hope. I left the dancing hall and planted myself near a whist table, where four experienced players were displaying great skill. I had become interested in watching the game, when a silvery laugh made my heart bound. Mary-Ann was behind me. I could not see her, I dared not turn toward her, but I felt her presence, and my joy was overwhelming. What was the cause of her mirth I never knew. Perhaps some ridiculous uniform; one meets such in every country at official balls. I remembered that there was a mirror in front of me. I raised my eyes and I saw her, without being seen, between her mother and her uncle; more beautiful, more radiant than on the day when she appeared to me for the first time. Three strands of pearls were around her neck and lay partly on her divine shoulders. Her eyes shone in the candle-light, her teeth glistened as she laughed, the light played in her hair. Her toilet was such as all young girls wear; she did not wear, like Mrs. Simons, a bird of paradise on her head; but she was not the less beautiful; her skirt was looped up with bouquets of natural flowers. She had flowers on her corsage, and in her hair, and what flowers, Monsieur? I give you a thousand guesses. I thought that I should die of joy when I recognized upon her the—Boryana variabilis. Everything came to me from Heaven at the same moment! Is there anything sweeter than to find

a coveted flower, for which one thought to search, in the hair of one whom one loves? I was the happiest of men and of naturalists. Excess of happiness made me cast to the winds all the proprieties. I turned quickly toward her, and holding out my hands, I cried:
"Mary-Ann! It is I!"
Will you believe it, Monsieur, she recoiled as if terrified, instead of falling into my arms. Mrs. Simons raised her head, so haughtily that it seemed to me as if her bird of paradise would fly away with it to the ceiling. The old gentleman took me by the hand, led me aside, examined me as if I was a curious beast, and said to me: "Monsieur, have you been presented to these ladies?"
"There is no question about that, my worthy Mr. Sharper! My dear uncle! I am Hermann. Hermann Schultz! Their companion in captivity! their savior! Ah! I have had some wonderful experiences since their departure! I will relate them to you at your house."
"Yes, yes," he replied. "But the English custom, Monsieur, exacts, absolutely, that one be presented to ladies before one relates stories to them."
"But since they know me, my good and excellent Mr. Sharper. We have dined more than ten times together. I have rendered them a service worth a hundred thousand francs! You know it well; at the camp of the King of the Mountains."
"Yes; yes; but you have not been presented."
"But do you not know that I have exposed myself to a thousand deaths for my dear Mary-Ann?"

"Very well! but you have not been presented."
"Present me, then, yourself."
"Yes, yes; but you must first be presented to me."
"Wait!"

I ran like a crazy man across the ball-room; I jostled several couples who were waltzing; my sword got entangled between my legs, I slipped on the waxed floor, and fell my full length. It was John Harris who helped me up.

"For whom are you searching?"

"They are here, I have seen them. I shall marry Mary-Ann; but I must be presented first. It is the English custom. Help me! Where are they? Have you not seen a large woman, with a bird of paradise head-dress?"

"Yes, she left the ball with a pretty girl."

"Left the ball! But, my friend, she is Mary-Ann's mother!"

"Be calm! we will find them again. I will have you presented by the American Minister."

"That is the very thing! I will show you my uncle, Edward Sharper. I left him here. Where in the devil has he hidden? He ought not to be far away!"

Uncle Edward had disappeared. I dragged poor Harris to the Place des Palais, before the Hotel des Etrangers. Mrs. Simons' apartments were lighted. At the end of a few moments the lights were extinguished. Everyone had gone to bed.

"Let us do the same," Harris suggested. "Sleep will calm you. To-morrow between one and two, I will arrange your affairs."

I passed a night much worse than those of my captivity. Harris slept with me, or rather, he did not sleep. We heard the carriages coming from the ball, descend Rue d'Hèrmes with their freight of uniforms and toilets. About five o'clock, weariness closed my eyes. Three hours afterwards, Dimitri entered my room and said:

"Great news! Your Englishwomen have gone!"

"Where?"

"To Trieste."

"Wretch! art thou sure of it?"

"It was I who accompanied them to the ship."

"My poor friend," Harris exclaimed, seizing my hands. "Gratitude may be assumed, but love does not come at will."

"Alas!" sighed Dimitri. This sentiment had an echo in his heart.

Since that day, Monsieur, I have lived like the beasts; drank, ate, breathed. I sent my collection to Hamburg without one specimen of the Boryana variabilis. My friends accompanied me to the French steamer the day after the ball. They thought it wise to make the journey during the night, for fear of encountering M. Pericles' soldiers. We arrived without accident at Piraeus; but when a short distance from the shore, a half-dozen invisible muskets sent their bullets singing about our ears. It was the pretty Captain sending his adieux.

I scoured the mountains of Malta, of Sicily, and of Italy, and my herbarium was much richer than I. My father, who had had the good sense to keep his inn, wrote to me, at Messina, that my efforts were appreciated. Perhaps I might find a place on arriving; but I determined to count on nothing.

Harris was en route for Japan. In one or two years I hoped to have news of him. The little Lobster had written me from Rome that he was still exercising with the pistol. Giacomo continued to seal letters all day and crack nuts at night. M. Mérinay found a new interpretation from the inscription on the monument, one more clever than mine. His great work upon Demosthenes ought to be printed some day or other. The King of the Mountains made peace with the authorities. He built a fine mansion on the road to Pentelicus, with a guard-house for lodging twenty-five devoted Palikars. In the meantime, he has rented a small hotel in the modern city, at the edge of the open sewer. He receives many people, and actively engages in public affairs, in order to be elected to the Ministry. Dimitri goes there occasionally, to supper, but sighs in the kitchen.

I have never heard of Mrs. Simons, of Mr. Sharper, nor of Mary-Ann. If this silence continues, I shall soon think of them no more. Sometimes, even in the middle of the night, I dream that I am before her and that my tall, thin figure is reflected in her eyes. Then I awake, I weep hot tears and I furiously bite my pillow. What I regret, believe me, is not the woman, it is the fortune and the position which escaped me. It is a good thing for me that I have not yielded up my heart, and each day I give thanks for my natural coldness. What I might complain of, my dear Monsieur, is, if unfortunately, I had fallen in love!

CHAPTER IX.

LETTER FROM ATHENS.

The day that I was about to send M. Hermann Schultz's story to the publishers, I received from the correspondent to whom I had sent the MS., the following letter:

Sir: The history of the King of the Mountains is the invention of an enemy of truth and the gendarmerie. No persons mentioned have set foot in Greece. The police have never vised any passports bearing the name of Mrs. Simons. The Commandant at Piraeus has never heard of The Fancy nor of Mr. John Harris. The Phillips Brothers do not remember of ever having employed Mr. William Lobster. No diplomatic agent has known any Maltese of the name of Giacomo Fondi. The National Bank of Greece has nothing with which to reproach itself, and it has never had on deposit, any funds made by brigandage. If it had received them, it would have considered it a duty to have confiscated them for its profit. I hold, for your inspection, the list of our officers of the gendarmerie. You will find no trace of M. Pericles. I know only two men of that name; one is a tavern-keeper in Athens; the other sells spices in Tripolitza. As for the famous Hadgi-Stavros, whose name I have heard to-day, for the first time, he is a fabulous being whom one must relegate to Mythology. I confess, in all sincerity, that there have been sometimes brigands in the country. The principal ones were destroyed by Hercules or Theseus, who may be considered as the real founders of Greek gendarmerie. Those who escaped the hands of these two heroes, have fallen under the blows of our invincible army. The author of the romance has displayed as much ignorance as dishonesty, in attempting to prove that brigandage exists to-day. I would give a great deal to have this romance published, may be in France, or in England, with the name and portrait of M. Schultz. The world would know by what gross artifices he has attempted to make every civilized nation suspicious of us.

As for you, Monsieur, who have always given us justice, accept the assurance of the kindest sentiments, with which I have the honor of being,

Your very grateful servant,
Patriotis Pseítis.

"Author of a volume of Dithyrambics upon the regeneration of Greece; editor of the Journal l'Esperance; member of the Archaeological Society of Athens; corresponding member of the Academy of the Ionian Isles; stockholder in the National Company of the Spartan Pavlos."

THE AUTHOR HAS THE LAST WORD.

Athenian, my fine friend, the truest histories are not those which have happened!

THE END.

www.ingramcontent.com/pod-product-compliance
Lightning Source LLC
Chambersburg PA
CBHW031738230426
43669CB00007B/397